RANGERS LEAD THE WAY!

TO BE A U.S. ARMY RANGER

Russ Bryant

ZENITH PRESS

First published in 2003 by Zentih Press, and imprint of MBI Publishing Company, 380 Jackson Street, Suite 200, St. Paul, MN 55101 USA.

MBI Publishing Company books are also available at discounts in bulk quantity for industrial or sales-promotional use. For details write to Special Sales Manager at MBI Publishing Company, 380 Jackson Street, Suite 200, St. Paul, MN 55101 USA

To find out more about our books, join us online at www.zenithpress.com.

ISBN 13: 978-0-7603-1314-5

Edited by Sara Perfetti
Designed by Stephanie Michaud

Printed in China

On the front cover: The assistant gunner of the M240G team feeds 7.62-millimeter ammunition into the machine gun.

On the back cover: (top) The RSOV from 2nd Ranger Battalion sits poised and ready for action. **(bottom)** Rangers conducting HALO operations.

On the frontispiece: A young Ranger is a team member of a squad of quiet professionals that can adapt and overcome any obstacle in their path. Rangers train and think as leaders, and can assume any leadership role in the squad if a man goes down. For this very reason, every Ranger has a working knowledge of all equipment, albeit communication, weapons system, or navigational aids.

On the title page: Rangers hustle to an Air Force MH-53 Pave Low for extraction after a live-fire raid exercise. The withdrawal is carefully coordinated with other aircraft to keep security in place until the Pave Low had lifted off. The AH-6 and MH-60-DAPs take gun runs on the smoking objective just in case hidden pockets of resistance emerge. Door gunners on the Pave Low are ready with fingers on triggers as well.

About the author/photographer:
Russ Bryant is a freelance photojournalist based out of Savannah, Georgia. His work has appeared in *Time* magazine, *The New York Times*, *Army* magazine, *Army Times,* and many other foreign and domestic print publications. Prior to earning his BFA in photography from the Savannah College of Art and Design, Bryant served in the 1st Ranger Battalion (B Company, 2nd Platoon) stationed at Hunter Army Airfield from 1985 to 1989. He was an enlisted member of weapons squad (M60 machine gun) and later an E-5/sergeant team leader. Bryant earned his Black and Gold Ranger Tab in Class 8-87. He now specializes in military photography.

CONTENTS

Dedication

This book is in memory of Sergeant Embry Trigg Langan
(1967–1992) B Company, 1st Ranger Battalion

This book is dedicated to Susan, my wife, best friend, and assistant
gunner, for her understanding, time, and devotion, which are all
inspiring to me. This book is for you.

Acknowledgments

It is difficult to convey the entirety and depth of my gratitude to those who selflessly lent a hand in my endeavor. I would like to thank the men of the 75th Ranger Regiment who, with truth, honesty, and dedication, have continued to embrace me as one of their own. Without their support over the years, this project would have never materialized. I am indebted to each and every one of them.

Monica Manganaro, Deputy Public Affairs Officer in Fort Benning, Georgia, was instrumental in guiding my plan of attack. Elsie Jackson assisted me greatly in determining whom to see, where to go, and when to be there.

Colonel P. K. Keen, past commander of the 75th Ranger Regiment, graciously showed a personal interest in my success. His support inspired me to continue with what I had begun.

Jeff Mellinger, past Command Sergeant Major of 1st Ranger Battalion, provided me with words of encouragement, and a ride or two, whenever our paths crossed.

A special thanks to: Colonel Joe Votel, Commander, 75th Ranger Regiment; Colonel (Ret.) Ralph Puckett, Honorary Colonel, 75th Ranger Regiment; Major Dan Walrath, Executive Officer, 1st Ranger Battalion; Major Erik Kurilla, 3rd Ranger Battalion; Lieutenant Colonel Kevin Owens, Commander, 2nd Ranger Battalion; Lieutenant Colonel Timothy J. Flynn, Commander 5th RTB; Command Sergeant Major Byron J. Barron, 5th RTB; Captain Charles Massarachia, Commander, B Company, 1st Ranger Battalion; First Sergeant John VanCleave, B Company, 1st Ranger Battalion; Colonel Hazen L. Baron, Commander, 4th RTB; Captain Matt Seifert, 1st Ranger Battalion; Captain Larry O. Basha, 3rd Ranger Battalion; Captain Eric Effiler, 1st Ranger Battalion.

Thanks to the personnel of the U.S. Army Special Operations Command Public Affairs Office: Lieutenant Colonel Walter E. Pierce, Major Andy J. Lucas, Carol Darby, Barbara Ashley, Staff Sergeant Amanda Glenn.

Thanks to Captain Larry Perino, 3rd Ranger Battalion; Colonel John S. Mosby, Ranger; Sergeant First Class Ken White, 5th RTB; Lieutenant Colonel Steve Hart, Public Affairs Office, Hunter Army Airfield; Timothy Hale, Public Affairs Office, Hunter Army Airfield; Sergeant First Class Lee Schmid, 1st Ranger Battalion; Captain Vincent Valley, 30th AG Battalion (Recruitment); First Lieutenant Scott Gilpatrick, 4th RTB; Master Sergeant Christopher Schott, 4th RTB; Staff Sergeant John Berlanga, 4th RTB; Command Sergeant Major (Ret.) Mike Martin; Captain Jeff Sacli, Commander, D Company, Airborne School; Mike Haenggi, MBI Publishing Company; Pete Nevis, MilSpec Group, Inc.; Bruce Zielsdorf, Chief PAO Army and staff, New York; First Lieutenant Jay Millen, Ranger School buddy, Class 8-87; Penny Neff; Sara Perfetti, MBI Publishing Company.

Special thanks extended to: R. David Duncan, III, a great photographer and friend who inspires me never to be satisfied; Michael Jordan, for his passion and drive to tell the military's story; Betsy Brairton, for her editing of text and her honest opinions; Amy Goodpaster-Strebe, colleague, reporter, writer, and dear friend; Sergeant (Ret.) Lee Michael Stacey, A Company, 1st Ranger Battalion, 1986–89, for leading the way with courage, leadership, resolve, and dedicated friendship; my family: mom and dad, brothers Kevin and Will, daughter Morgan, and son Travis.

With deepest gratitude and appreciation: Adonis Mouna and Nazar Mouna at PhotoMaster, Savannah, Georgia, for color processing and printing of the images; Alex Gilmore, Bay Camera Company, Savannah, Georgia, for equipment support; Alice Gabriner, *Time* magazine, for photo editing and contact sheets; support provided by the Kodak Professional, a division of the Eastman Kodak Company, and Laurie O. Bernard; Airborne Girl Productions, Columbus, Georgia; Viper Images Inc., Savannah, Georgia; MilSpec Group, Inc., Reno, Nevada; Nikon Professional Services; Leica Professional Services; Savannah College of Art and Design, Savannah, Georgia.

New recruits pledge their loyalty to God and Country as members of their assigned Basic Training company.

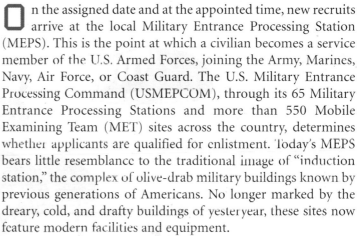

FROM CIVILIAN TO SOLDIER

On the assigned date and at the appointed time, new recruits arrive at the local Military Entrance Processing Station (MEPS). This is the point at which a civilian becomes a service member of the U.S. Armed Forces, joining the Army, Marines, Navy, Air Force, or Coast Guard. The U.S. Military Entrance Processing Command (USMEPCOM), through its 65 Military Entrance Processing Stations and more than 550 Mobile Examining Team (MET) sites across the country, determines whether applicants are qualified for enlistment. Today's MEPS bears little resemblance to the traditional image of "induction station," the complex of olive-drab military buildings known by previous generations of Americans. No longer marked by the dreary, cold, and drafty buildings of yesteryear, these sites now feature modern facilities and equipment.

The MEPS staff uses a series of evaluations and interviews to determine each applicant's qualifications for enlistment. During 2001, approximately 272,068 young people met the standards for service in the armed forces. However, if our national security were to be threatened, and the armed forces were required to mobilize, the number of people processed by the MEPS would quadruple.

The arriving recruits bring with them only the items on their military-endorsed packing list, a document devoid of most personal items. In the weeks ahead, there will be little time for recreation. They will spend their leisure time recuperating from the taxation of body, mind, and spirit.

At the MEPS, administration checks the details of the recruits' personal information. Before MEPS staff members administer the Oath of Enlistment, they fingerprint recruits for an FBI check and perform a pre-enlistment briefing and interview. Background screenings of applicants are also important. These include Entrance National Agency Checks to confirm United States citizenship as well as the absence of drug usage, sexually deviant behavior, financial irresponsibility, and membership in organizations dedicated to overthrowing the U.S. government. In addition, applicants must attest to not having relatives or close friends living in certain designated countries.

The enlisting officer conducts the Oath of Enlistment exclusively in English. Enlisting soldiers are given the option to swear or affirm and may omit the phrase "so help me God." Visitors and family members may attend and photograph the ceremony. Individual enlisting soldiers may even have their photograph taken with the enlisting officer following the event.

0900 hours. The room is full of young men preparing to enter the U.S. Army. They fill out the reams of paperwork, then go to the finance department to receive their $200 advance. Afterward, each new enlistee completes a Last Will and Testament.

The Armed Services Vocational Aptitude Battery (ASVAB) tests are part of the qualification process for the armed services. They are the result of more than 50 years of research and are nothing like the army's old "Alpha" and "Beta" tests of World War I, which were written tests that assisted recruiters in determining whether a student would be best suited as an officer or as an enlisted soldier. The MEPS command administered 581,264 enlistment ASVAB tests nationwide during 2001. Many examinees take this test through their high school guidance department in their junior or senior years. The ASVAB is available as a "paper and pencil" test at the Mobile Examining Team sites and as a Computerized Adaptive Test at the Military Entrance Processing Station sites. The ASVAB is a multiple-choice test that helps identify which army job, referred to as Military Occupational Specialty (MOS), is best suited for each enlistee. It is not an IQ test. It measures knowledge and ability in ten areas, from math to electronics. There is no passing or failing score on the ASVAB, but to be considered for enlistment in the army, one must earn a minimum of 31 points.

Keeping to the high standards of the U.S. Army, a young recruit assures that his appearance is perfect. The recruit polishes his boots with a boot brush, black polish, and an old-fashioned wad of spit.

In 2001, more than 530 Mobile Examining Team physicians administered 389,242 medical examinations to applicants. A complete medical examination consists of a physical examination, a clinical interview, and lab work. Generally, height, weight, and body fat percentages are measured; hearing and vision acuity are evaluated; orthopedic and neurological functions are screened; and blood/urine is tested for the HIV antibody, sickle cell anemia, and abnormal sugar levels. The thorough nature of these examinations is to help ensure applicants can meet the physical challenges of military service.

There are some disqualifying conditions that applicants are allowed to correct before commencement of service and other conditions that prohibit them from service altogether. Generally, recruiters advise and counsel applicants regarding disqualifying conditions prior to any enlistment agreement. At the MEPS, a complete medical history, which encompasses past and current conditions, is obtained by a medical technician. In many cases, a medical condition is not an automatic reason for exclusion from military service and instead requires further evaluation or a previous doctor's recommendation. However, under a newer Department of Defense directive, a history of asthma is a disqualifying condition for initial military service, as asthma almost always reoccurs during training, flaring up especially during intense early-morning exercise. The military can disqualify from service any applicants that are prescribed such medications as insulin or oral hypoglycemic agents, anticonvulsants, antiarrhythmics, anticoagulants, antihypertensives, and digitalis preparations. Some disqualifying conditions are specific to the branch of service and the occupation specialty requirements.

In addition to the standard requirements for entry into the regular army, there are specific medical health fitness standards for the initial selection to airborne and Ranger training. For example, the applicant must demonstrate nothing less than full strength, stability, and range of motion for all joints. The applicant must not have a history of vertigo, persistent tinnitus (ringing or buzzing in the ear), or limited movement of the eardrum. For each soldier, an electrocardiogram (EKG) is administered to check the health of the heart. The prospective airborne or Ranger soldier must be able to distinguish between the colors red and green. Distant visual acuity must be correctable to 20/20 in one eye and at least 20/100 in the other eye. Lung function must be normal. Chest x-rays are sometimes conducted. Soldiers must exhibit normal emotional responses to stressful situations and demonstrate emotional stability. Functions of the head, neck, and spine must be normal, as the physical demands of the airborne and Ranger

Rarely does anyone talk, joke, or tell stories in this barbershop. It is so quiet that the men can hear large clumps of hair hitting the floor between the droning whir of electric shavers.

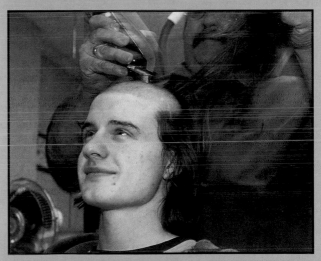

Uncle Sam takes your $4.00 and gives you the cheapest haircut ever, and you get more than your money's worth. Many young men have sat in these chairs and then walked away looking like new people.

training will test the strength of these areas. Chronic motion sickness, a fear of flying, an attempted suicide, or a history of psychosis would be conditions for exclusion from airborne or Ranger training.

The number of precautions the military takes during MEPS processing illustrates a key point. In order to protect their own lives and the lives of others around them, it is vitally important that the soldiers present top physical fitness. Presenting anything less would be a hazard.

Basic Combat Training (BCT)

Now the transformation from civilian to soldier begins. A bus transports the soldiers to the place of Basic Combat Training (BCT). Recruits are assigned to one of five posts conducting Basic Training. Each post specializes in different MOSs, which determine the assigned location for training. Locations are Fort Benning, Georgia; Fort Jackson, South Carolina; Fort Leonard Wood, Missouri; Fort Knox, Kentucky; and Fort Sill, Oklahoma. Many refer to this training as simply "Basic." All who enlist in the army are required to complete this eight-week course. The training received here is the basis for all other training the soldiers will receive, regardless of their choice of MOS.

The first week is Reception Week, a time for soldiers to arrive and get settled in their new living quarters. It takes approximately three duty days to "in-process" the new soldiers. In-processing entails giving soldiers haircuts and issuing them physical training (PT) uniforms, initial uniform clothing, linens, and a handbook. This handbook contains the procedures and standards for operating as a U.S. Army soldier, including how to wear the uniform, salute an officer, operate a weapon, and more. Soldiers have their uniform nametags and alterations ordered. The army issues each of them an identification card and tags called "dog tags," which soldiers wear every waking moment. The identification card is necessary for entrance into dining facilities, stores, and services within the military post as well as onto secured military bases. Soldiers are given several briefings. Toward the week's end, the army conducts the first of many physical training tests. The soldiers must complete an 8.5-minute mile, along with push-ups, pull-ups, and sit-ups. Army instructors teach the young soldiers the basics of barracks upkeep—wall lockers are neat and orderly with clothing articles specifically folded or hung on hangers, beds are made without the slightest visible crease, and bathrooms are so clean that they appear unused—as such maintenance details promote discipline, responsibility, and teamwork. Learning marching drills, addressing others, saluting, and caring for and wearing of the uniform prepares them for the drill sergeant.

The first week of BCT consists of classroom instruction on drill and ceremony, which includes everything from saluting to walking and marching in parades. The drill sergeant, usually a staff sergeant or sergeant first class, easily commands the attention and respect of all those around him. He may appear absent of humor, but he possesses strong values. The U.S. Army's seven core values are loyalty, duty, respect,

At Basic Rifle Marksmanship training, soldiers wait in line to move to the ammunition point. Something distracts a young trooper's attention. This infraction results in additional PT for him and more push-ups later, just to remind him that one does not move the head when at attention.

A drill sergeant intently focuses on the rifleman's shot during Basic Rifle Marksmanship training at Fort Benning, Georgia. The Colt M16A2 is the standard, basic training issue rifle for all, regardless of their gender and MOS. To pass Basic Combat Training, soldiers must earn qualifying marks. Once soldiers are assigned to their permanent duty station, they may be assigned a different weapon system.

selfless service, honor, integrity, and personal courage. New soldiers first learn of these values in the classroom, but beginning with BCT's second week, training moves from the classroom to the field, where challenges are waiting.

Each soldier develops teamwork with an assigned buddy. The idea here is that an individual soldier does not succeed at a task alone; his respective buddy must succeed as well. Basic first-aid classes equip the buddies with knowledge of how to care for a wounded soldier until medical personnel arrive. Together soldiers learn map reading, land navigation, and compass usage. They practice what has been taught on a land navigation course, during which the buddy teams attempt to move from one point to the next according to the given azimuths, directions, and distances. Those who do not complete the course correctly just might be late to the chow hall. Drill sergeants demonstrate hand-to-hand, or unarmed,

combat; then the soldiers practice accordingly. It is not until the third week that the army entrusts a rifle in the hands of these new soldiers.

Basic Rifle Marksmanship (BRM) encompasses everything the operator needs to know about the weapon, a standard issued Colt M16A2. It is one of the most combat-proven weapon systems in the world. The M16A2 rifle is a 5.56-millimeter caliber, lightweight, gas-operated weapon capable of semi-automatic and fully automatic operation. When properly zeroed and operated, it has a range of 1,000 meters (1,094 yards). Proper maintenance is crucial. After instruction and rehearsal, soldiers have three minutes to disassemble and reassemble the rifle. Drill sergeants teach soldiers every part's name and function, and soldiers must recite these upon request. To pass the marksmanship tests, soldiers must be able to hit a stationary target at a distance of 100 feet. Soldiers

Soldiers prepare to advance to the firing line to qualify with the weapon. The three levels of rifle marksmanship are sharpshooter, marksman, and expert, with the latter as the ultimate goal. These trainees are already designated as 11-series MOS (infantry) and will spend a great deal of time on rifle ranges throughout their military service.

must also hit pop-up targets at distances of 20 feet, 50 feet, and 100 feet.

This third week of training presents mounting physical and mental challenges. This is the week the physical training demands increase to a 5-kilometer (3.1-mile) foot march. Frequently, buddies will encourage and challenge each other in order to complete this run within 45 minutes.

The sight of "The Chamber" casts an aura of uneasiness in some soldiers and downright fear in others. It is the Nuclear Biological Chemical (NBC) training that mentally taxes these already tired recruits. Drill sergeants send soldiers one by one into a chamber containing CS gas, a nonlethal but poisonous tear gas used in battle to drive enemies from their bunkers. While inside, the soldiers must remove their masks and clearly pronounce their names, ranks, and Social Security numbers to the monitoring drill sergeant,

who, by the way, is fully protected with a mask. Talking without protection causes the foul gases to fill the lungs. The soldier must then replace the mask and clear it by blowing, an act similar to that of clearing a snorkel of water. One by one, the soldiers exit the other end of the chamber, but unlike their calm and orderly entry, they come running out with teary eyes and runny noses, and are coughing uncontrollably. The gas burns not only their faces and bodies, but also sears the experience into their minds forever.

An obstacle course is the setting for the fifth week. Each buddy team must negotiate and clear up to 20 obstacles while running and jumping, climbing and vaulting, traversing and crawling. The obstacles include walls and rope ladders to climb, balance beams and bars to cross, and hurdles and poles over which to jump. The course usually requires the teammates to swing on ropes and crawl under barbed wire as well.

With his back covered in mud, a soldier continues on the bayonet assault course. Soldiers learn how to negotiate the obstacles with their rifle and bayonet without getting tangled up in the barbed wire. Earlier in the day, classes were given on the proper fighting techniques, including stroke, slash, and parry. Soldiers are taught how to fall with the bayonet without causing injury to themselves or fellow soldiers.

The bayonet assault course requires soldiers to go up and over barbed wire, wade through water, jump ditches, climb walls, and attack tires. The course's length is approximately 250 yards, and when the soldiers are not "double-timing" it, they are low-crawling. To show extra motivation, recruits let out a big yell.

No one leaves the course until completely covered with mud. The Basic Combat Training instructors will gladly see to this. And no one leaves the course alone. Buddy teams assist one another, but the soldiers must complete this timed event as a squad. The squad is only as good as its slowest person.

The soldiers have made it halfway through BCT, but the training is not yet over. During the next weeks, teamwork is expanded as the soldiers work in a squad, a platoon, and a company unit.

The highlight for the next week is an extensive obstacle course that recruits must negotiate with their company. This untimed course shows recruits how far they have come and how well Basic Training has prepared them for the army. It gives them confidence in their mental and physical abilities and cultivates their "spirit of daring." It underscores the importance of teamwork and unity. The recruit's confidence has culminated in an improved self, platoon/company, and army.

The confidence building continues with 10-kilometer (6.2-mile) and 15-kilometer (9.3-mile) foot marches and a 3-day field exercise that provides the soldiers with an understanding of what combat can really be like. Live fires with M-60 rounds blasting overhead combined with a conglomeration of artillery and small arms fire create a battlefield atmosphere. Much of this is conducted during the night, as the company's mission is to secretly infiltrate an enemy post. The experience exemplifies just how far the soldiers have come and what lies ahead.

A company of apprehensive basic training soldiers prepares for an unforgettable experience in the gas chamber at Fort Benning, Georgia. Once the soldiers are instructed, geared up, and inside the building, the drill instructor waits several seconds before ordering them to remove their masks. It does the soldiers no good to hold their breath, because the drill sergeant will make them talk before ordering them to walk out of the building. Sometimes the stinging tear gas makes recruits close their eyes while exiting. Some nearly walk into a tree.

(next pages) Marching in formation and across a painted infantryman's crest, these men receive their blue cords and will wear light-blue disks behind the U.S. and crossed rifle insignias.

AR 670-1: The Army Regulation "six-seventy-dash-one" explicitly sets the standard on how to wear the U.S. Army uniform. It specifies the proper measurements between each award and decoration as well as the order in which they must appear on the uniform. In earlier years, soldiers wore their awards and decorations just about anywhere and rarely measured anything. They just "eyeballed it." As years went by, the standards tightened and everything was measured with rulers. For a mere 99 cents, recruits can purchase templates that explain how to get their pins and ribbons perfectly in place.

Burning and tearing eyes, extreme burning in the nose and throat, stinging skin, mucus secretion through the nose, uncontrollable coughing, involuntary closing of the eyes, slowed breathing and heart rate, and an increase in blood pressure are expected reactions to the gas chamber's 0-chlorobenzalmalononitrile, more commonly referred to as CS. CS is actually a white, powdery compound that is mixed with another agent, such as methylene chloride, to make the particles airborne.

In this particular Basic Combat Training class, the 4th Platoon consists of 40 highly motivated men with the "Ranger" option on their recruiting contracts. After Basic Combat Training graduation, they attend Advanced Individual Training, Airborne School, and Ranger Indoctrination Program as a unit. These men will know each other well by the time they complete this 20-week training regime and receive their Ranger Battalion assignment. Grouped as a "test" platoon reminiscent of an earlier training structure, these men develop uncanny motivation and teamwork.

Family members are warmly encouraged to attend the "Turning Blue" ceremony and Basic Combat Training graduation. This is the first time loved ones have seen their soldier in nine weeks. **Respective family members are asked to place the blue infantryman's cords on the soldier's uniform. The drill sergeant, who has been a surrogate mother and father for the past two months, proudly awards cords to those without attending family. After the company commander's speech, the men are allowed a 48-hour pass to spend time with family and friends.**

Teamwork means "squaring away" your buddy. The squad members check the closeness of a shave as they prepare for a walk-through inspection by the drill sergeant. These pre-designated, 11-series MOS soldiers are in their Class-A uniforms for the "Turning Blue" ceremony, the awarding of the light-blue infantryman's cords which are to be worn on the right shoulder. From this ceremony, the soldiers directly report to their Basic Combat Training graduation.

(below) "Airborne!" Five jumps must be completed in order to graduate from the U.S. Army Basic Airborne Course. Fryar Drop Zone at Fort Benning, Georgia, is home to the "Black Hats," who conduct Jump School. Infantrymen are transformed into paratroopers. The men implement airborne standard operating procedures on the ground before moving to the elevated apparatuses. All Rangers are airborne-qualified.

A student is suspended in a harness to gauge the weight of his body in a parachute. He learns to pull the riser slips, which steer or direct the parachute into the wind before landing. This "leg" has the toggles of a "dash 1-C" parachute.

ADVANCED INDIVIDUAL TRAINING (AIT)

Following BCT graduation and after spending time with family, new soldiers bid farewell to one another. They leave for various training facilities to begin Advanced Individual Training (AIT), which is specific training according to their Military Occupational Specialty (MOS). Enlistees generally choose their MOS at the time of enlistment, so there are few surprises when the soldiers receive their training orders. AIT is designed for each of the military occupations: cook, mechanic, clerk, engineer, medic, field artillery gunner, radio operator, and so on.

The AIT for the infantryman is the next step for the soldier on his way to one of the three Ranger Battalions.

Today's infantry soldiers are smart and very well trained. They use hand-held computers to collect and relay information about the positions of both their unit and the enemy to their commanders miles away, all in near real-time. Technological advances are created and tested continually, and provide infantry soldiers with cutting-edge training and equipment. Before long, they will carry powerful laptops in their rucksacks that pinpoint positions and perform equipment diagnostics. Even the weapons they carry will be computerized. These advances are vitally important when ground troops conduct missions in urban environments. In these cases, to say such equipment saves lives is no understatement.

Basic Airborne Course (BAC)

The airborne infantrymen proceed to the Basic Airborne Course (BAC), otherwise known as Jump School or Airborne School. Since its inception in the early 1940s, Eubanks Field at Fort Benning, Georgia, has served as the sole location for Jump School. The purpose of the three-week BAC is to train the volunteer in the use of the parachute as a means of combat deployment. Through mental and physical conditioning, the course also helps students to develop leadership skills, self-confidence, and an aggressive spirit. To put it simply, Airborne School is a school of confidence and leadership.

Soldiers must be physically fit before the start of BAC. The physically weak are more likely to not complete the course because of an injury or to fail the course due to an inability to complete the training apparatuses. Physical training (PT) is the first period each day and is followed by seven hours of demanding, vigorous training. The airborne cadre, the select group of officers and enlisted men who train the airborne infantrymen, recommends that each volunteer engage in PT prior to BAC entrance. With this training, soldiers should be able to complete a 5-mile run in 45 minutes or less after executing 30 minutes of strenuous endurance and muscle-strengthening exercises. To qualify for entry into Jump School, the soldiers must successfully complete three events: push-ups, sit-ups, and a 2-mile run. They must earn a minimum score of 180 points out of 300, or a minimum of 60 points per event, using the 17- to 21-year-old age group requirements scale on the Army Physical Fitness Test (APFT). Regardless of age, volunteers must meet and maintain these minimum standards. Furthermore, the entrant must be no older than 36 years of age. Finally, all enlisted personnel entering BAC must have completed Basic Combat and Advanced Individual Training or other approved equivalent training.

The U.S. Army has bestowed upon the 1st Battalion (Airborne), 507th Infantry Regiment, the responsibility of conducting Airborne School. The Airborne School instructors are the world-renowned "Black Hats" and are from the U.S. Army, U.S. Marine Corps, U.S. Navy, and U.S. Air Force. They train students in the use of the static line deployed parachutes. The 1st Battalion is organized into six companies: the Headquarters and Headquarters Company is in charge of administrative actions as well as command and control; four Line Companies (A, B, C, and D) execute the BAC Program of Instruction (POI); and Company E provides parachute rigger support. The same platoon sergeants, section sergeants, and squad leaders train their students during the three training phases: Ground, Tower, and Jump. This structure and teaching philosophy strengthens unit cohesion, teamwork, discipline, and supervision. The end result is to have quality paratroopers throughout the U.S. Armed Services.

The swing-landing trainer (SLT) helps evaluate mastery of the different parachute landing falls (PLFs). An airborne instructor controls the apparatus without telling the students which way they will approach the land. Landings are graded as satisfactory or unsatisfactory. By the day's end, the students are covered in sand from the landing pit. Those meeting success continue the Basic Airborne Course.

With a rush of wind and adrenaline, the student glides down from the 250-foot towers at Jump School. In this controlled setting, the student perfects canopy control and landing technique. Although not its purpose, the tower tests one's nerve.

Trainees must qualify daily during PT by completing a set of specified exercises, which typically includes stretching warm-up exercises, calisthenics maintenance exercises, and a 3- to 4-mile formation run. Any student who fails to complete at least two of the five daily runs per week will be eliminated from training. The average pace is 9 minutes per mile. This policy treats all BAC students as equals and meets current XVIII Airborne Corps standards. Soldiers encourage and challenge one another, which builds teamwork and camaraderie.

The first week of BAC is called Ground Week, as much of the trainees' time is spent learning how to hit the ground. The students learn the parachute landing fall (PLF) to land safely in the drop zone. The concept is to land with feet and knees pressed together. The flawless PLF has five sequential points of contact to absorb shock of impact: balls of the feet, calves, thighs, buttocks, and push-up muscles, or back loin. When in the air, paratroopers desire to turn into the wind and land facing forward, but they sometimes find themselves drifting to the side or backwards instead.

Trainees must practice PLFs from different directions: front, back, front left and right, back left and right, and so on. In practice, the airborne students jump off a table into a sandy pit. Using structures that resemble the C-130 and C-141 aircraft, the trainees learn the proper method to exit the aircraft. A 34-foot tower with a lateral drift apparatus allows the students to practice proper body positioning for exiting the aircraft and landing. With instructors nearby to evaluate every move, trainees have ample feedback and opportunity to practice these techniques repeatedly.

The second week of training is called Tower Week, which continues the daily physical training each morning. During Tower Week, trainees refine the individual skills learned during Ground Week. The "mass exit" concept is added to the training. The apparatuses used this week are the 34-foot towers, the swing-landing trainer (SLT), the mock door for mass exit training, the suspended harness, and the 250-foot free tower. This tower allows airborne candidates to practice controlling the parachute while descending from 250 feet. They must learn how to handle parachute malfunctions, as

The mock door exit resembles the paratroopers' passageway from an aircraft. The students rehearse exiting the aircraft and counting, "One thousand, two thousand, three thousand, four thousand, five thousand," before checking the canopy and gaining control. The paratrooper must look out for the other jumpers and check the rate of descent.

At the 34-foot tower, a "Black Hat" grades and critiques the student exiting the mock door. The tower is just high enough to give the student the feeling of being "airborne" when exiting. Because it lacks the fierce wind and deafening noise, this is merely a timid approximation of a real jump.

Roster numbers are the form of identification used during Airborne School.

A "Black Hat" instructor talks to airborne students about the five points of performance. The reserve parachutes are painted with distinctive red paint so they are never rotated into active service unless, of course, to be used in activities for which they were intended. The students use old and disabled silk parachutes during Ground Week.

twisted risers or partially inflated canopies can mean trouble and require immediate correction. Tower Week completes the individual skill training and develops teamwork. To go forward to Jump Week one must qualify on the SLT, master the mass exit procedures from the 34-foot tower, and pass all PT requirements.

The final week of Airborne School is Jump Week. Successful completion of the previous weeks of training prepares the soldiers for Jump Week. During the first two weeks, the students learned how to gain control over their parachute canopies and how to guide their parachutes by pulling toggles to direct themselves toward the drop zone (DZ). The airborne candidates must now master a variety of jumps: day and night, individual and mass exit, with and without equipment, and jumps using various round-canopied parachutes. Usually, the course culminates with a mass tactical jump at a 500-foot altitude from a C-130 onto Fryar Drop Zone. Upon completion of this jump, the students assemble in formation, march to the assembly area, and go through a graduation ceremony.

Graduation is normally conducted on the Friday of Jump Week at the south end of Eubanks Field on the Airborne Walk. Guests and family members are welcome to observe all of the jumps at the drop zone, attend the graduation ceremony, and participate in awarding the wings. Graduating soldiers, especially those with a military family tradition, may have someone from their family pin on their silver Jump Wings.

Ranger Indoctrination Program (RIP)

Once a soldier completes Basic Combat Training, Advanced Individual Training, and Airborne School, the next training step is the Ranger Indoctrination Program, which has the foreboding acronym RIP. RIP is a three-week program for

enlisted soldiers in grades E-1 to E-4. All Rangers are three-time volunteers: first in the army, second in Airborne School, and then in the Ranger Battalion. The mission of the Ranger Training Detachment (RTD) that conducts RIP is to prepare, assess, and select the soldiers for service in the 75th Ranger Regiment. The purpose of RIP is not only to provide the soldier with the tactical skills to function as a member of a Ranger squad, but also to eliminate the weak and unmoti-

vated. Unfortunately, the rest of the RIP class suffers from the mistakes and attitudes of the unmotivated. The RIP cadre consists of non-commissioned officers who are carefully chosen from the 75th Ranger Regiment. These instructors have firsthand knowledge of how to function as a Ranger squad member. They know that the Ranger squad is only as strong as its weakest member. Weakness in body, mind, and spirit will cost lives. It may appear that the cadre implements

Most students learn the Ranger Creed prior to arrival, as each is required to recite it daily at PT formation.

On the first day of training, students must receive a minimum of 70 points out of 100 in each area on the Army Physical Fitness Test. Regardless of their age, students are required to perform according to the 17- to 21-year-old age group requirements. Also included in the Ranger Physical Fitness Test is the pull-up event. As if the APFT is not challenging enough by itself, the RIP cadre will ensure all of the students' major muscle groups are adequately worked before the APFT is even administered. Water operations are in the trainees' future if they become Rangers, so success on the Combat Water Survival Test (CWST) is also a must. The soldiers must be able to swim 15 meters (49.2 feet) while wearing Battle Dress Uniforms (BDUs), boots, and load-carrying equipment (LCE). Once candidates pass these two crucial events, the AFPT and CWST, the real training, or "smoking," begins.

The training cadre may provide a brief overview of RIP to the incoming enrollees, but day-to-day training is not spelled out as it is done in such programs as Basic Combat Training and Airborne School. Rangers need to develop flexibility in thinking so they can effectively and efficiently confront any situation as it arises. Therefore, the Ranger candidates are kept guessing as to what is going to happen during every hour of rigorous training for the next three weeks.

The Ranger candidates are under the constant supervision of the RIP cadre, especially when military skills are being taught. The cadre begins instruction by teaching regimental history, lineage, tradition, and standards. Rangers have seen combat in every major conflict that has involved the United States. The Ranger lineage and longstanding history of tactics practiced in actual conflicts have become the basis for all other U.S. Special Operations Forces.

For those soldiers of grades E-5 and above, a similar-type program is designed. It is known as the Ranger Orientation Program (ROP) and is managed and conducted by the Ranger Training Detachment at Fort Benning, Georgia. Upon ROP graduation, the noncommissioned officers report directly to the Pre-Ranger Cadre to begin in the next Pre-Ranger Course. The physical challenges at orientation are nothing compared to what lies ahead. Before infantry noncommissioned officers can report to a Ranger Battalion, they must be Ranger-qualified. In other words, all NCOs must get through Ranger School to earn the elusive black and gold Ranger Tab.

punishments regardless of whether a soldier makes mistakes or performs well. It might be difficult to determine if anyone truly performs well at RIP, but any properly motivated soldier can pass and become a U.S. Army Ranger.

The Ranger Training Detachment (RTD) located at Fort Benning, Georgia, conducts the RIP training. Day Zero allows students to arrive, sign in, and pick up their bed linens. The first day starts at 0450 hours, with soldiers in PT uniform.

After the successful completion of the Ranger Indoctrination Program, this platoon of 40 men graduates with pride at the Ranger Memorial outside Infantry Hall at Fort Benning. This is the first time these men are officially authorized to wear the tan Ranger beret. Most of these Rangers are assigned to the 1st Ranger Battalion, the next Ranger Battalion on rotation for Ready Reaction Force. Although they can now wear the tan beret and the Ranger Battalion scroll, they are not yet true Rangers. They still have a lot to learn, and until they do, they are called "cherries" and "newbees."

The cadre conducts airborne operations to familiarize the men with Ranger Regimental Airborne standards and procedures. They learn that assembling after a jump in an airborne unit and assembling as a Ranger Battalion are two very separate and distinct activities. They also learn map reading and advanced land navigation skills. They practice these skills, and then the cadre evaluates them on both day and night land navigation courses.

The entry level tasks the men learn at RIP are more advanced and extend beyond their AIT instruction. Rangers

The RIP cadre will ensure that each soldier is physically challenged. Some may coin this as "motivational" physical training. At the command of the instructors, it is common for trainees to stop whatever they are doing, drop to the ground, and knock out push-ups. The RIP cadre will readily provide a candidate with a large rock to put in his rucksack if he finishes a run first or without a sweat. For practicing "fireman" carries, the cadre appears to possess an uncanny ability to quickly size up trainees and partner each man with someone who is at least 30 pounds heavier than he is. A few years ago, Cardiac Hill was a favorite after a long run. As the nickname would imply, Cardiac Hill on Fort Benning can get the heart pumping, muscles burning, and lungs stinging. Its incline is at an approximately 45° angle. Just imagine a southern summertime run with 98 percent humidity.

do not operate in a basic manner by any stretch of the imagination, and their training reflects this. Discipline and teamwork are underscored throughout this training process. In addition, the proper equipment maintenance is stressed—lack of care and maintenance now is a recipe for disaster later.

The entry-level tasks include assisting in the performance of reconnaissance operations, locating and neutralizing mines, and operating and maintaining communications equipment. In situational training exercises, RIP instructors teach and evaluate infantry dismounted battle drills. The trainee must learn to operate, mount, dismount, zero, and engage targets using night-vision sight equipment. The cadre also teaches how to construct field-expedient firing aids for infantry weapons; how to successfully operate in an NBC-contaminated area with the proper equipment; how to process prisoners of war and captured documents; and how to master the fundamentals of fast-roping.

Basic First Aid training in AIT and Basic Combat Training was just that: basic. But now, much more is required of these soldiers. They need to be able to administer more extensive emergency care until medical personnel can intervene. The resulting Combat Lifesaver certification training includes treating shock, hypothermia, and heat exhaustion; applying a tourniquet; treating chest wounds or extensive bleeding; executing CPR and artificial resuscitation; and administering an

After the "Dawning of the Tan Beret," a family member or team member pins on the Ranger Battalion scroll. Rangers explain, "The Ranger Tab is a school. The Ranger scroll is a way of life." The colorful black and red Ranger Battalion scroll is for the Class-A uniform. A tactical, olive-drab scroll is worn on the everyday uniform.

IV. The army's "learning by doing" approach leaves some soldiers poked and bruised from practicing with IV needles.

Candidates prove to themselves and the cadre that they can perform as members of a Ranger squad. Intrinsic motivation and an unwavering desire to become the best are the two underlying traits soldiers need to possess in order to pass RIP and become a Ranger. However, to be considered a success and a graduate of RIP, the Ranger candidates must accomplish a 5-mile run at a pace of at least 8 minutes per mile and complete a 10-mile road march plus their choice of either a 6- or an 8-mile march. Exam scores must be 70 percent or above.

According to some sources, RIP's attrition, or drop-out, rate is somewhere between 25 percent and 40 percent. This failure rate is somewhat dependent on such things as weather and time of year. In the summer months, the average daily high temperatures in Columbus, Georgia, climb above the 90°F mark with high relative-humidity readings. This results in excessive heat index measurements. Thunderstorms and tornadoes are not uncommon. Temperatures in the winter months are relatively mild, generally recording around 35°F, but occasionally storms cause icy conditions. Regardless of the weather, some soldiers find the road marches extremely challenging and are unable to complete the marches within the allotted time.

But for those who do graduate from RIP, the experience offers a heightened and well-deserved sense of accomplishment. Upon RIP graduation, each Ranger enlistee is awarded his Tan Beret and is assigned to one of the three Ranger Battalions or to the 75th Regimental Headquarters. They are permitted to sew the scroll of their assigned battalion onto their uniforms. From this moment, the Ranger Scroll becomes a way of life.

RANGER SCHOOL

Candidates must pass a stringent orientation course before selection to U.S. Army Ranger School. Once enrolled, they'll face the kinds of physical and mental challenges that will serve as a foundation for membership in one of the army's elite combat units. Upon graduation from Ranger School, they will receive the signature black and gold crescent-shaped tab—a symbol that only those who wear it can truly comprehend.

Rigorous screening by the 4th Battalion Medical Section precedes entrance to Ranger School. Ranger students must have complete medical and dental records, and undergo a Ranger School physical within the 12 months prior to entry. All personnel must bring a complete set of health records to Ranger School. This includes a current dental Panorex film (X-ray) or a statement of its availability. If there is any discrepancy in the records, a lack of records, or a documented disqualifying condition, the student will not be allowed to participate in the course.

Prior to entrance, Ranger School students receive two medical briefings. The first explains what medications and personal medical care items may and may not be brought to Ranger School. The second briefing's content is referred to as the "medical threat" and covers poisonous insects, plants, and animals; heat and cold injuries; and other assorted illnesses and injuries that may affect Ranger School students during training. And finally, the Ranger students are each given two shots at inprocessing (initial processing) to Ranger School, a procedure that began in the early 1990s. As a result of the rigorous training, the immune system becomes depressed, making these shots necessary. Provided they are not allergic to penicillin, the students will receive shots of Bicillin-L-A and Pneumovax 23, which guard against pneumonia and other possible infections.

The mission of Ranger School is to conduct Ranger and long-range surveillance leader courses. These courses are meant to further develop the combat arms skills of officer and enlisted volunteers who are eligible for units in which the primary mission is to engage in the

On an open field during Ranger Assessment Phase (RAP), Ranger School candidates stand at "parade rest" while attentively receiving a block of instruction. Their eyes focus intently upon the Ranger instructor's every move.

close-combat, direct-fire battle. Despite any traditional leadership skills students may derive, Ranger School specifically purports *not* to be a leadership course, per se; such skills are a secondary benefit.

The examination of the true boundaries of human potential in relation to the actual level of human effort exerted is the essence of the course's philosophy. Ranger instructors acknowledge that the typical comfort zone for effort amounts to less than 25 percent of true human potential. The Ranger School students self-impose enough effort to reach 50 percent of total human potential. The Ranger School course imposes a stress level that stretches students to reach 75 percent of their possible potential. Reaching the maximum of 100 percent human

(above) Going into the Central Issuing Facility (CIF) for equipment issue, Ranger School candidates stand in a tight, single-file line. So tight, in fact, many patrol-cap bills touch the heads of the men in front of them.

potential would mean total exertion, or death. Therefore, Ranger School instructors are well trained and experienced in evaluating the level of each student's potential, stress threshold, and exerted effort.

The backbone of the Ranger School program is the Ranger Instructor, or RI. One hundred percent of the instructors are Ranger-qualified, meaning that they have completed Ranger School themselves. They possess leadership experience and have an average of two to four years in leadership positions. Ranger instructors generally have two to four years of college education and must complete a three- to six-month instructor certification process. These instructors are also experienced

(right) These students are "getting smoked" by the RI since they did not move as quickly as they could or should have moved. Students always have a time deadline to meet, and they usually miss it. Timeliness is at the RI's discretion. Students frequently run everywhere, as walking is interpreted as lack of motivation (LOM). The RI shouts, "Are you ready to quit, slugs?" A Ranger School student can quit at any time.

in combat; many are veterans of combat in Grenada, Panama, Somalia, Kuwait, or Iraq. In addition to Ranger School training, these individuals have also completed other specialized training, including Jumpmaster and High Altitude Low Opening (HALO) schools; Pathfinder; Basic Non-Commissioned Officers Course (BNCOC) and Advanced Non-Commissioned Officers Course (ANCOC); Scuba; Air Assault; Survival, Evasion, Resistance, Escape (SERE); Assault Climber; Advanced Mountaineering; and Emergency Medical Training (EMT) and Combat Lifesaver.

The Ranger Training Brigade (RTB) conducts the Ranger School in three phases: the "Benning Phase" at Camp Darby and Camp Rogers, located at Fort Benning, which is near Columbus, Georgia; the "Mountain Phase" at Camp Merrill, located near Dahlonega, Georgia; and the "Florida Phase" at Camp Rudder, located at Eglin Air Force Base, which is near Fort Walton, Florida. The Benning Phase is at Brigade Headquarters and has an estimated 44 instructors. The 5th Ranger Training Brigade at Camp Merrill has approximately 162 Ranger instructors. And Camp Rudder's 6th Ranger Training Brigade has 170 instructors. The course's length of 61 days is divided among the three phases: Benning Phase for 20 days, Mountain Phase for 21 days, and Florida Phase for 18 days. The remaining two days are consumed by travel between the phases, maintenance, in/out processing, and graduation. The Ranger Training Brigade trains for 348

The Ranger School instructors receive ample food and sleep, besides regular physical training. They are known for their muscular mass and endurance, but more importantly for their experience and leadership.

Early in RAP, each Ranger School student is assigned a roster number. It is by this number that APFT and CWST scores, spot and incident reports, and peer and patrol evaluations are maintained. The roster number is prominently displayed on the Kevlar helmet.

days out of the calendar year, and 310 of these are considered high-risk training days.

The 61-day Ranger School is a long and rigorous course. The bodies of the Ranger students weaken as the course progresses, making mental toughness essential. Over the span of the course, Ranger School students each carry a 35- to 55-pound "Alice pack," or backpack, and conduct tactical foot movements of 200-plus miles, a distance similar to that between New York City and Boston. Although the average soldier consumes 2,800 to 3,200 calories daily, Ranger students eat no more than 2,200 calories a day and expend every bit of this fuel, and then some. It is common for students to lose 20 to 30 pounds of body weight. Since these men average 19.6 hours of training each day, seven days a week, the Ranger students can expect no more than four hours of sleep each night. The highest attrition is during Ranger Assessment Phase (RAP) week. The common problem areas in RAP week are the APFT, CWST, the 5-mile run, and Land Navigation. Ranger School graduation statistics for 1991–2000 indicated an average graduation rate of 56.3

Visual reminders of each candidate's quest are displayed time and again throughout each Ranger training camp. Black and gold Ranger Tabs are hung from buildings, obstacles, and towers; are suspended from arched entrances to fields and training areas; and are plastered on the chest of every RI.

Prior to the RAP knife-fighting classes, the students are briefed by the RIs. The highly motivated students sound-off before being paired up.

percent. The average graduation rates for 2000 and 2001 were around 52 percent.

The Ranger Training Brigade has developed a comprehensive program to reduce the number of students who drop out of Ranger School. The plan to reduce the attrition rate includes controlling the number of students reporting to Ranger School in the first place and targeting only leaders in the designated MOSs outlined in The Army's Chief

Since the Ranger Course's birth in 1951, Ranger instructors have trained over 35,000 students from the U.S. Armed Forces and military personnel from some 60 allied countries. Units that contribute to a typical Ranger School class include:

75TH Ranger Regiment
Ranger Training Brigade
82ND Airborne
101ST Airborne (Air Assault)
10TH Mountain Group
25TH Infantry Division (Light)
173RD Airborne Brigade
172ND Separate Infantry Brigade
Heavy Divisions
Special Forces Groups
Navy
Air Force
Marines
Foreign Armies

Equipped in a Kevlar helmet and LCE, a student sounds-off loudly during rifle PT. He holds the rifle out in front while doing a deep squat. Total muscle failure is common during grueling exercises. When this occurs, an exercise that targets a different muscle group is ordered.

(next pages) After passing under the arched entranceway topped with the black and gold Ranger Tab, the candidates enter the hand-to-hand combat pit. They run the pit's perimeter with rifles held high overhead before receiving their first instruction block of bayonet training.

(left) Quads and abs burn mercilessly for those not in top physical condition before entering Ranger School. At some point, muscles will ache and burn for even those in superb shape. Physical exercises include low-crawling, duck-walks, flutter-kicks, turn-and-bounce, and the painful dying cockroach, as seen here.

"Your individual weapon will be with you at all times." The weapon accompanies the Ranger School candidate during mop detail in the barracks. A loss of weapon, even while billeted in the barracks, leads to negative consequences for the individual as well as for his team and squad leader. Accountability for personnel and equipment is always expected.

(right) During pre-dawn PT, students execute the "turn-and-bounce" upper arm and shoulder exercise at the RI's count. To execute this move, arms are outstretched to the side with palms facing upwards. Moving from the waist, the right shoulder is turned to the rear, and the left is turned to the front for a count of three. The arms and torso return to front and center, then the turning move is reversed with the left shoulder leading.

of Staff Attendance Policy dated April 1997. The policy can be summarized as follows: Officers come from infantry, armor, air defense artillery, cavalry, fire support, field artillery, special forces, and combat engineering units. Units must be routinely attached to or in direct support of infantry battalions to be a designated and approved MOS. Enlisted soldiers who are in these MOSs can attend: Infantry-man; Indirect Fire, Heavy Anti-armor Weapons, and Fighting Vehicle Infantryman; Combat Engineer, Fire Support Specialist, and Avenger Crewman from units that directly support infantry battalions; Special Forces Personnel; Cavalry Scout; and Armor Crewman. Those enlisted soldiers of any MOS or specialty assigned to Ranger-coded positions within the 75th Ranger Regiment or Ranger Training Brigade may also attend, meaning that even the cook at a Ranger Battalion's dining facility could attend Ranger School. Students may originate from all branches of the U.S. Armed Services and foreign ally armies.

The process to reduce the attrition rate begins at the sending unit's level. Commanders recommend only the best soldiers from their units for Ranger School selection. Each unit has a limited number of slots for the Ranger School class, and commanders use these slots carefully. This fosters a spirit of competition among many, but also camaraderie. A squad's "tabbed" superiors are performing well at their jobs if their subordinates are well trained and ready for Ranger School. Unit commanders are ultimately responsible for ensuring that applicants are in top physical condition and knowledgeable of combat infantry tasks, as applicants are returned to their units if the entry requirements are not met. The failure of an applicant is a direct reflection upon the unit and its commander. For many, this is simply unacceptable.

A typical Ranger School class of 250 or so students generally earns an APFT score of 280 or above, which exceeds the minimum 210-point requirement. The student age-range is 19 to 27 years with an average 2.3 years of military experience. Officers comprise approximately 40 percent of a typical Ranger class, while the remaining 60 percent are enlisted and non-commissioned officers. Usually, soldiers

Early on in Ranger School, students secure pieces of luminous tape to the back of their patrol caps (PCs) and rucksacks. This permits the Rangers to see and follow a fellow Ranger at night, thus avoiding a break in contact. These "cat eyes" are secured in a specific way. Using a needle and some dental floss, each of the square's corners is secured with a square knot followed by two half-hitches. If executing this task late at night after an exhausting day, tired minds and fingers can spend an hour or so to complete it. In Ranger Battalions, the shape of the tape signifies the Rangers' company affiliation.

need a rank of Specialist (E-4) or above, but Ranger School sometimes grants slots to those having a Private First Class (E-3) rank and 12 months of service in the Ranger Regiment or Battalion. Typically, 40 percent of a Ranger class graduates with its original class without recycles.

In Ranger School, the attrition rate for Battalion Rangers is less than 10 percent. This may be partly due to the constant military training these Rangers undergo on a daily basis. It also may be partly the result of the Pre-Ranger Course for Battalion Rangers, which is a one-month course consisting of physical conditioning as well as basic skills training in patrolling and ambushes. During the Pre-Ranger Course training, students receive ample food and sleep.

The Army National Guard Bureau has staffed the two-week Pre-Ranger Course with National Guard cadre who are Ranger School graduates and veterans. Some have prior service with the 75th Ranger Regiment and/or Ranger Training Brigade (RTB). The course is under the command of the 4th RTB and is another aspect of the comprehensive program to reduce attrition. This Pre-Ranger Course (PRC) is conducted eight times a year and is open to all soldiers who qualify for Ranger School attendance, including those from both active and reserve units. The first week tests soldiers on RAP tasks, and the second week is "Zero Week" for Ranger School.

Graduates of the PRC have a much higher chance of moving on to Ranger School than those who do not attend the course. In 1999, for example, the success rate of the course graduates was 70 percent greater than the success rate of active-duty soldiers.

Zero Week, the week prior to the Ranger class starting date, is an optional program conducted by the 4th RTB of Fort Benning. According to Zero Week program statistics, completion of the program lowers the rate of attrition during the first seven days of Ranger training. Zero Week's intent is to produce soldiers who are prepared to enter the first day of the Ranger course. Zero Week is not intended to make soldiers proficient in any single task. It is conducted to reinforce previously mastered skills. Also, Zero Week allows soldiers to become more acclimated to the Georgia weather. Some soldiers may be traveling

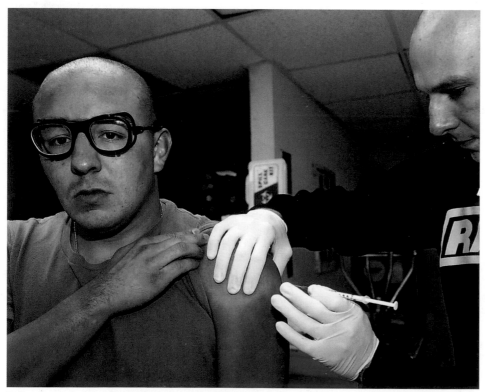

Before moving on past the Ranger Assessment Phase (RAP), the students line up to receive the required dose of penicillin. The Ranger Training Brigade (RTB) is conducting an ongoing study to see if fewer bacteria-related illnesses occur during the course as a result of this preventive measure.

across several time zones or from a drastically different climate and need time to adjust before undergoing the physical and mental stress that lies ahead. Plus, oftentimes there are variables in travel orders, so Zero Week gives ample time for the students to arrive.

Approximately 90 percent of the Ranger School students attend Zero Week. During this week, the training cadre administers physical fitness and swim tests. Students who successfully complete the APFT and CWST during Zero Week do not repeat these tests during the beginning of Ranger School. Those soldiers who do not meet the minimal scores on the APFT and CWST are allowed another opportunity to achieve a passing performance during the Ranger Assessment Phase (RAP). Program instructors conduct daily physical training during Zero Week. Before selection to Ranger School begins, students already know link-up and reconnaissance, passage of friendly lines, ambushes, patrol base, fragmentary orders, operation and warning orders, basic land navigation and map reading, and time management. Zero Week is a time to review these aspects of conducting a mission. Finally, Ranger students receive their immunizations. At Zero Week's end, students generally receive a 24- to 48-hour pass to get away one last time before they "crawl" through the first training phase.

Incoming Ranger students bring all of their required uniforms and equipment. The list of required items is extensive and specific. Students must have name tags as well as the inscription "U.S. Army" sewn on their uniforms, but they must remove all rank and unit insignia. Regardless of rank, students are addressed as "Ranger." They are not to wear starched fatigues. Only unmodified regular army-issue boots are authorized, and any student with forethought will break in these boots prior to Ranger School.

The list of what is allowed and what is not allowed in Ranger School addresses more than just attire. It states that letter writing and religious reading materials are permitted. Tobacco products are not allowed. As the students learned in an earlier briefing, medications, including over-the-counter vitamins, are not permitted. Contact lenses may not be worn. Students are permitted and encouraged to bring lip balm, sunscreen, non-aerosol insect repellent, foot powder, and a first-aid dressing. Students report to Ranger School with closely cropped "high and tight" haircuts, as hair is believed to complicate good hygiene. More frequently, students shave their heads completely. Ranger camps have a limited number of showers, hand-washing facilities, clothes washers, and dryers.

Pay telephones are available throughout the three phases of training, except at Camp Darby. However, it is unlikely that students will have any significant time to make casual phone calls. When it comes to written communication, the Ranger School issues all mail received within the Ranger Training Brigade to the student. The members of the cadre are not permitted to open any mail addressed to a student; they can, however, certainly require a student to open a suspiciously bulky or padded letter in their presence. If students open letters containing chocolate bars or sticks of gum, good sense will tell them to surrender the contents. Ranger students are discouraged from receiving packages while they are in training. All packages received for students are held until the end of the field training exercises (FTX). Frequently, Ranger students send wish lists of desired food to their wives, girlfriends, or mothers, then anxiously await packages filled with chocolate bars, cookies, and brownies, which they will receive at the end of the course. Unauthorized "junk" foods are defined as any foods not found in a Meal Ready to Eat (MRE) or served at a designated meal.

Black leather gloves, glove inserts, L-shaped flashlight, dog tags, ID card, foot powder. Candidates hold their equipment up high during a check so the RI can see that everything is there and in its place. All students begin with the same equipment, affording them equal footing and resources.

The quest for the Ranger Tab has begun.

As noted earlier, the first seven days of Ranger School make up the Ranger Assessment Phase (RAP), which assesses each individual's level of readiness to participate in the Ranger training. This is conducted at Camp Rogers in the Old Harmony Church area at Fort Benning, Georgia. Students who successfully complete RAP will remain in training. Individuals who do not readily demonstrate proficiency in the course prerequisites during RAP are released and returned to their units. Those failing re-tests may be offered the opportunity to "recycle," or start over with the next Ranger class. Re-tests and recycles are not automatic and are dependent on both the approval from the sending unit and the availability of slots.

Students must pass the APFT, consisting of push-ups, sit-ups, and a 2-mile run in running shoes. Despite the students' actual ages, the new standards require that all students meet the minimum requirements for the 17- to 21-year-old age group. This requires 49 push-ups, 59 sit-ups, and a 2-mile run completed within 15 minutes, 12 seconds. In addition, applicants must do six chin-ups with palms turned toward the face.

Since much of the Florida Phase consists of water operations, students must also pass a swim test. The CWST

The six chin-ups for the APFT are the first of many chin-ups executed over the coming days. On Malvesti Field the men must contend with wet, muddy hands on slippery metal bars. Before permitted to move out, the squad must execute the pull-ups in unison according to the RI's command.

consists of three stations: the 15-meter (49.2-foot) swim, the 3-meter (9.8-foot) drop, and equipment removal. In the interest of safety, the swim test occurs in a swimming pool with medics nearby who are certified in water life-saving and life-saving apparatus. During the 15-meter swim, each applicant must wear BDU, boots, and carry a rifle and LCE. The LCE consists of a pistol belt, suspenders, two ammunition pouches, and two full canteens. The equipment and clothing alone weighs approximately 25 pounds when dry. The swim must be conducted without loss of the rifle or any equipment and without showing fear or panic.

The 3-meter drop requires the student to walk blindfolded off a 3-meter diving board with a rifle and LCE. After entering the water, he must remove the blindfold and swim to the pool's side without loss of rifle or equipment and without showing fear or panic.

The final task, equipment removal, requires the student to enter the water from the poolside and submerge by himself. He must then discard his rifle, remove his LCE,

and make sure that it is totally free from the body before resurfacing and swimming back to the poolside. Naturally, this must be conducted without showing fear or panic.

During RAP week, the training cadre evaluates the applicants' strength and endurance. All students must complete a 5-mile formation run on a hard surface and over a rolling terrain while wearing running shoes. This formation run is set at a pace of eight minutes per mile, and the run must be completed in 40 minutes or less. The second strength and endurance run is the 16-mile tactical foot-approach march. Students must complete the tactical foot march at a rate of 2-1/2 miles per hour, which is the army's approved march rate. This translates to a range of 17 to 21 minutes per mile. Students must march with a 40-pound rucksack if it is winter and a 35-pound rucksack if it is summer. The march is conducted on surfaced and unsurfaced roads, both with rolling hills. Instead of running shoes, the students wear boots. Applicants get one chance at each test; should they fail either the 5-mile run or the 16-mile march, they are returned to their original unit.

The night and day land navigation test is a combination course. The test commences in the dark, early-morning hours and concludes in the daylight. Students must locate the required number of stakes within the prescribed time period to receive a passing grade, or a "go." This is a pass or fail evaluation, but in this case students may be re-tested. On an individual basis, students must earn five out of six possible points. The course spans 4 to 5 kilometers (about 2.5 to 3.1 miles) and must be completed within five hours. During Zero Week, the training cadre reviewed basic aspects of land navigation and map reading; here, the students demonstrate their knowledge of these basics or chance a recycle.

RAP week is not yet over. Students must also demonstrate their skill at tying knots. Knot-tying is used during each of the training phases, and lives and equipment depend upon the near-instinctual knowledge and ability to quickly and correctly tie knots. In the weeks to come, students need to determine which knots to use in a variety of situations.

Although they are graded on many specific skills, the Ranger students must also be proficient in a variety of areas for which they are not formally evaluated. A good working knowledge of these non-graded tasks increases their probability of succeeding in Ranger School.

The RIs grade and record specific criteria each student must master in order to arrive at Ranger School Graduation Day and have the black and gold tab pinned upon his left shoulder. Although each student is evaluated individually, his academic record reflects his capacity for teamwork. Students must pass, or receive a "go," on at least 50 percent of their graded patrols. They must

During the CWST, an RI pushes a student backward into the pool. While treading the deep water, the student submerges and removes his LCE and weapon, letting them sink to the pool floor. If the student resurfaces with either the LCE or weapon, he is a "no-go" and must be re-tested.

Prior to walking out on the land navigation course, students need a full working knowledge of how to execute the following tasks :
1. Navigate from one point on the ground to another point while dismounted
2. Determine the grid coordinates of a point on a military map
3. Determine a magnetic azimuth using a lensatic compass
4. Determine the elevation of a point on the ground using a map
5. Determine a location on the ground by terrain association
6. Measure distance on a map
7. Convert azimuths
8. Determine azimuth using a protractor
9. Orient a map using a lensatic compass
10. Orient a map to the ground by map/terrain association
11. Locate an unknown point on a map and on the ground by intersection
12. Locate an unknown point on a map and on the ground by resection

pass at least one combat patrol operation in each phase. On average, each Ranger student is graded on one patrol at the squad level during the Benning Phase and two patrols at the platoon level in both the Mountain and Florida Phases. Students are in a graded position when designated as the platoon sergeant, platoon leader, or assistant platoon leader. One of these graded combat patrol operations must be in a primary leadership position (e.g., platoon leader or platoon sergeant). A student who does not pass is graded as a "no go."

Each student's abilities are continuously evaluated throughout the Ranger Course, not solely during the graded patrols. RIs assess students based upon how effectively they influence and motivate their subordinates and

The RI assists a student in preparation for the CWST, reminding the student of the graded task points and what he must do to receive a "go" at this swim test station.

Eating on the run takes on a new meaning. Hungry students hang their heads low while shoveling in food with a spoon. There is no time for forks and knives.

A Ranger School student attentively listens to the RI explain the proper assembly of the Kevlar helmet, its chinstrap, and airborne retention strap. Note the Leatherman tool that he is using. It is a square, flat tool containing a knife, pliers, flat and Phillips screwdrivers, corkscrew, and fingernail file. This tool will see a lot of action throughout the Ranger course.

how well they use available resources in accomplishing all assigned tasks and missions.

At the end of each phase, peer evaluations are conducted, during which the Rangers grade each other according to predetermined criteria. The RI collects this data and counsels the "peered" students. On a student's first peer failure, he is moved to a new squad. On his second peer failure, he may be reassigned, recycled, or dropped from the course. If a soldier is peered a third time, he is generally dropped from the course and returned to his unit. A score of 60 percent on each peer evaluation must be attained in order to receive a "go."

Critical Incident Reports (CIRs), or spot reports, can be either positive or negative, and are quick evaluations conducted at the moment that behavior has occurred. They are a method of evaluating student performance primarily in a non-graded position. Major and minor positive spot reports are awarded for high motivation, initiative as a squad member, exemplary team work, and superior performance as a team leader. Examples of actions that would result in a minor negative spot report include not having one's weapon on "safe," having unsecured equipment, and sleeping at an unauthorized time. RIs give a major negative spot report if a student accidentally discharges his weapon or if they need to make repeated minor spot corrections with an individual. Excessive negative spot reports result in a board review. The board decides what further action should occur, such as a recycle or removal from the course. Spot reports are cumulative from phase to phase. Three minor spot reports are equivalent to one major spot report. Any major or minor positive spot report cancels out a major or minor negative spot report and vice versa.

The fourth method of evaluation is the Special Observation Report (SOR), which is reserved for violations of the most serious nature. These include safety violations, chain-of-command violations, and honor violations like lying, stealing, or cheating. Depending upon the seriousness of the violation, SOR violations can result in a drop from the course, return to the parent unit, and the likelihood that the student will never be granted the opportunity to attend Ranger School again.

At the end of each phase, the battalion chain of command responsible for that specific phase reviews academic records to determine each student's eligibility for remaining in the course. If a

On a breezy, clear day, the airborne-qualified Ranger candidates participate in a refresher jump at Fryar Drop Zone during RAP. This is a static line jump from an altitude of approximately 1,500 feet using the C-130 and C-141 aircraft.

"Getting smoked" during RAP is all part of the process. A Ranger School candidate grimaces and pumps out push-ups on the graveled company area. Outside the barracks is an area where the men assemble for PT, equipment checks, inspection, instruction, or any other reason for which the RIs need the entire company present.

student's performance is substandard, the battalion commander makes a decision of removal, recycle, or continuation for that student. The Ranger Training Brigade Commander is the highest reviewing authority.

The 4th RTB surgeon (right) administers first aid to real-world injuries sustained by Ranger School candidates during the refresher jump on Fryar Drop Zone, Fort Benning. High winds during the C-130 aircraft's first pass caused one student (left) a mild concussion and a second to possibly dislocate his shoulder. Neither injury was serious, and both students were inserted back into the course.

THE BENNING PHASE

The Benning Phase of Ranger training is also referred to as the "Crawl Phase." It is designed to assess the students' physical endurance and stamina. Those men who are not in top physical condition will experience significant difficulty maintaining the accelerated pace of Ranger training. The Benning Phase is also designed to further develop the military skills, mental endurance, and personal confidence soldiers must have to successfully lead and accomplish combat missions. The experiences the Ranger students encounter during this phase will teach them how to properly

sustain themselves and their men, and how to maintain equipment while coping with difficult field conditions.

Camp Robert Rogers, Fort Benning's Ranger-training camp, owes much of its warrior philosophy to its namesake. During the French and Indian War of 1754 to 1760, soldier Robert Rogers developed the warrior concept to an extent never known before. Operating in the days when commanders personally recruited their men, he was articulate and persuasive and knew his trade. Rogers had a magnetic personality. He expounded upon the natural abilities of the frontiersmen by organizing tactics similar to guerilla warfare. His rate of success was undeniable. Rogers published a list of 28 commonsense principles, known as Standing Orders for Rogers' Rangers, which stressed operational readiness, security, and tactics.

The Benning Phase is executed in two parts. The first part is conducted at Camp Rogers in the Old Harmony Church area of Fort Benning, Georgia. This phase consists of the RAP for the first week. Ranger students must also complete a 3-mile run with an obstacle course; take a medical considerations class; master terrain association, demolitions, and patrol base; and learn objective rally

"Cooperate and graduate. You can't do it alone," states the RI as he counsels students. Completing Ranger School is not a one-man operation or an individual endeavor. It is a team effort. There are tasks that cannot be done alone. Every Ranger student is paired with another, and the two must be together at all times for the next 60 days. They eat, sleep, run, and train side by side. Perhaps most importantly, they sustain and motivate each other. A unified Ranger buddy team will persevere with tenacity and dedication. Ranger buddies meet during the first days of Benning Phase and often remain friends for life.

The morning sun just breaks the horizon as the highly motivated Ranger students enter the hand-to-hand combat pit during RAP week. If the RI cadre senses that the students are not motivated for training, the candidates are ordered to leave the pit and do the training over again.

Flushed from exertion and glistening with sweat after pre-dawn PT, these Rangers endure the southern heat and humidity. They also endure the biting sand-gnats and mosquitoes. It may be difficult to rise before the sun, but that may be the only time of day the bugs are still asleep.

point and rifle, bayonet, pugil stick, and hand-to-hand combatives tasks. For those who are airborne-qualified, RIs conduct a refresher jump at Fryar Drop Zone. The advanced physical training assures physical and mental endurance. Pre-dawn runs are common as are countless push-ups, flutter kicks, and turn-and-bounce. Stamina is important as it enhances the basic Ranger characteristics, which are critical for successful Ranger School completion.

The Malvesti Field obstacle course begins with pull-ups and a run of about 50 yards then progresses to the obstacles with more pull-ups and running between each apparatus. The first obstacle on Malvesti Field is a vertical ladder that stands approximately 30 feet high. The Ranger must raise himself from the lower log to an upper one until he reaches the top and can climb over and down the other side. The challenge is that the logs are spaced increasingly farther apart as they progress upward. The Ranger students also negotiate an overhead, horizontal ladder to cross a water-filled pit. Falling in the pit means starting over, which increases the challenge as the students are wetter and muddier than when they started.

Malvesti Field is named in honor of Colonel Richard J. Malvesti, who made many contributions to the development of today's Rangers. He served many assignments, including Ranger instructor in Florida Phase; Company Commander, Battalion S-3, and Battalion S-4 at 2nd Ranger Battalion; Commander, Executive Officer, and Deputy Commander of Delta; and Assistant Operations Officer and J-3 at Joint Special Operations Command. Malvesti made the ultimate sacrifice in the service of his country. He died in a parachute accident on July 26, 1990, at Holland Drop Zone, Fort Bragg, North Carolina.

The cargo-net obstacle is a long climb up thick ropes to the log at the top then down ropes on the other side. Its structure resembles an A-frame. The savvy Ranger student will stand on ropes near the top, reach over the log, and grab rope on the opposite side. He will then flip his body over the log in a somersault fashion, thus benefiting from gravity to help him negotiate the downward side. Low-crawl is the method of movement through the "Worm Pit," a watery, muddy pit encased with barbed wire strung low to the ground. The pit is approximately 1-1/2 feet deep and 200 feet long. This obstacle assists Ranger School students to overcome any natural hesitation to enter a physically uncomfortable situation.

Additionally, the students complete the Water Confidence Test at Hurley Hill, also known as Victory Pond. Ranger students must climb a ladder to a 30-foot-long suspended log that they then walk across. At the log's end, they shimmy, or "commando crawl," on their bellies to cross on a rope until they reach a wooden, black and gold Ranger Tab hanging from the rope. The Ranger students must sound-off in a loud voice and ask the RI for permission to drop. Only when allowed will the students let go and drop approximately 40 feet into the pond. Then it is out of the water again to climb a 60-foot

tower. Once at the top, the Ranger students grab hold of a slide apparatus attached to a steel cable that is stretched over Victory Pond. The students then begin their descent, a 120-foot-long "slide for life." Upon the RI's signal, they dismount into the water. A fear of heights or water will demolish any chance of completing these obstacles. This test is required unless the water temperature is below 39°F or the wind chill factor is below 38°F. Only the lucky "Chosen Frozen," soldiers enrolled in the wintry months, will escape a swim in Victory Pond.

Camp Darby, a densely wooded and hilly area of Fort Benning, is named in honor of William Orlando Darby. Darby was appointed as the first commander of the 1st Ranger Battalion, activated on June 19, 1942. He organized and trained carefully selected men to lead key World War II missions in places like North Africa, Tunisia, and Italy. His record of success astounded military leaders, who bestowed upon him the task of training two additional Ranger Battalions, the 3rd and 4th. His active participation in these units led to the honorary nickname of the 1st, 3rd, and 4th Ranger Battalions, which are known as Darby's Rangers.

The second part of the Benning Phase is conducted at Camp Darby. Students live and operate in the woods

STANDING ORDERS FOR ROGERS' RANGERS

1. Don't forget nothing.
2. Have your musket clean as a whistle, hatchet scoured, sixty rounds powder and ball, and be ready to march at a minute's warning.
3. When you're on the march, act the way you would if you was sneaking up on a deer. See the enemy first.
4. Tell the truth about what you see and what you do. There is an army depending on us for correct information. You can lie all you please when you tell other folks about the Rangers, but don't never lie to a Ranger or officer.
5. Don't never take a chance you don't have to.
6. When we're on the march we march single file, far enough apart so one shot can't go through two men.
7. If we strike swamps, or soft ground, we spread out abreast, so it's hard to track us.
8. When we march, we keep moving till dark, so as to give the enemy the least possible chance at us.
9. When we camp, half the party stays awake while the other half sleeps.
10. If we take prisoners, we keep 'em separate till we have had time to examine them, so they can't cook up a story between 'em.
11. Don't ever march home the same way. Take a different route so you won't be ambushed.
12. No matter whether we travel in big parties or little ones, each party has to keep a scout 20 yards ahead, 20 yards on each flank, and 20 yards in the rear so the main body can't be surprised and wiped out.
13. Every night you'll be told where to meet if surrounded by a superior force.
14. Don't sit down to eat without posting sentries.
15. Don't sleep beyond dawn. Dawn's when the French and Indians attack.
16. Don't cross a river by a regular ford.
17. If somebody's trailing you, make a circle, come back onto your own tracks, and ambush the folks that aim to ambush you.
18. Don't stand up when the enemy's coming against you. Kneel down, lie down, hide behind a tree.
19. Let the enemy come till he's almost close enough to touch, then let him have it and jump out and finish him up with your hatchet.

—Major Robert Rogers, 1759

When billeted in the barracks during the Benning Phase, Rangers store their equipment in wall lockers. Maintaining the wall lockers and accounting for equipment are indications of the students' readiness.

At Malvesti Field, students low-crawl through the muddy water during the seemingly endless physical training. To clear the barbed wire's sharp spurs, students must submerge or carefully turn their head to the side.

(above) Between crossing the monkey bars and executing chin ups, students lie on their backs pumping out flutter-kicks or pounding out jumping jacks. This provides the Ranger instructors ample time to make sure the students really desire to be in the course.

Ranger training at Fort Benning, Georgia, began in September of 1950 with the formation and training of 17 Airborne Ranger companies during the Korean War. In October 1951, the U.S. Army Infantry School established the Ranger Department and extended Ranger training to all combat units in the U.S. Army. The first Ranger class for individual candidates graduated on March 1, 1952. On November 1, 1987, the Ranger Department reorganized into the Ranger Training Brigade and established four Ranger Training Battalions.

(left) Across a road and approximately 200 yards away from the 4th RTB's Headquarters lies Fort Benning's Malvesti Field. The area is part grassy field and part long, shallow pool of mud. Both sections have obstacles. The water is stained an orangey-brown from the red Georgia clay.

without the benefit of buildings. The emphasis at Camp Darby is on the instruction in and execution of squad combat-patrol operations. The Ranger students receive instruction on the fundamentals of patrolling, the warning order/operations order format, and communications. Camp Darby covers such tasks as battle drills, ambush and reconnaissance patrols, drills on how to enter and clear a room, airborne operations, and air assault operations.

These skills enable the soldier to conduct successful combat-patrol operations. The Ranger students practice the techniques first, then they must demonstrate their

(above) Ranger School students conduct mountain climber exercises in the muddy water between obstacles. Ranger buddies bellow out their count in unison. This is a four-count exercise that focuses on the leg muscles.

Rangers move at full speed with unprecedented motivation. Up and out of the muddy "worm pit," these candidates run to the chin-up bars.

(right) To properly execute a flutter-kick, the men first lie on their backs. They place both hands palms down, side-by-side under the buttocks and raise their legs from the hips to an approximate 45°-angle to the ground. Their knees are slightly bent. Their shoulder blades remain in contact with the ground, and the head is off the ground. They then alternate legs in a scissoring motion without feet or legs touching the ground.

(below) Victory Pond is pivotal to a Ranger's life. This is where soldiers begin and end Ranger School. They will return to this site during subsequent training with their Ranger Battalion. For some, their first introduction to Victory Pond is at Basic Combat Training. Here, Rangers await their chance to climb the tower, walk the log, crawl along the rope, and then ask the RI's permission to drop before releasing their grip.

During the Water Confidence Test, this student sounds-off loudly to the RI below. He wants to be certain that he is heard so he will not need to hang onto the rope any longer than necessary.

(inset) On Fort Benning's Darby Queen obstacle course, the Ranger student quickly scales the 20-foot cargo nets. At the top, he grasps the rope and actually flips over the wooden log securing the ropes, then slides down the same ropes on the opposite side.

There is a specific procedure for negotiating each obstacle on the Darby Queen course. Parallel black and gold two-by-fours are mounted on an A-frame. The students climb on their backs, over and under each of the boards. On the decline, they turn on their backs and descend headfirst, over and under the boards again. This obstacle is called the Weaver.

expertise through a series of tactical patrol operations led by RIs and then led by individual students. The Rangers conduct these operations during a 12-day field-training exercise over rugged terrain. The average "tactical foot movement," or distance traveled by foot, is 4 kilometers (about 2.5 miles). The After Action Review (AAR) is a verbal discussion between the commander and those conducting the mission, and assists with the learning process. Rangers quickly realize that mission planning is essential if they are to conduct successful reconnaissance and ambush patrol missions. The Benning Phase's end result is a Ranger with greater tactical and technical proficiency who is therefore better prepared to advance to the next Ranger School training phase. He moves from "crawling" to "walking."

Caked sawdust and dirt cover this Ranger student's face as he quickly scoots through the cement pipe, one of the many obstacles on the Darby Queen course. Ranger buddy teams must complete the course within minutes of each other.

This obstacle requires the Commando Crawl across a rope. At the other end, students must swing off and away from the pit below the rope.

On the Darby Queen obstacle course, students vault onto a log, then briskly walk along it to the monkey bars. If these Rangers have not yet developed callused hands, blisters are guaranteed. Falling off the log or bars means the students must retry the obstacle.

THE MOUNTAIN PHASE

Camp Merrill took its name in honor of a World War II hero, Major General Frank D. Merrill. During a campaign in Southeast Asia in 1944, Merrill and his "marauders" distinguished themselves by climbing mountains, crossing rivers, and maneuvering through jungles to surprise the enemy. These men fought sickness and exhaustion as well as the Japanese. The U.S. Army disbanded the group after fighting for three months and losing 80 percent of its 3,000 volunteers to disease and combat. Years later, smaller Ranger units were formed in the Korean and Vietnam conflicts. And in 1973, General Creighton Abrams authorized a battalion-sized Ranger unit, which grew to over 2,000 men by 1984.

Camp Merrill is located in the North Georgia Mountains, within the 100,000-acre Chattahoochee National Forest.

The Appalachian Mountain Range may not have the altitude of the Rockies, but its heavily forested and rocky geography provides a challenging, rugged terrain for training. The camp shows the wear of having housed thousands of soldiers since its start in 1959. Among the tall pines are the planning, or staging, areas numbered with painted, wooden markers.

A row of hutment called "hooches" once bordered the area. Built in 1961, these served as student billeting (lodging for soldiers) for many years. They are now demolished—with the exception of one for posterity's sake. Hooches were marginally better than the bare ground and open air. Resting upon cinder-block pillars, these huts had wooden-plank walls and floors. Over the years, the wind whistled through the ever-increasing number of gaps in the walls and floor. Tin roofs affected by

Linked in pairs, Ranger buddies complete the Darby Queen course together. For this task, the students perform alternate leg lunges in a trench between the obstacles.

weather and age leaked unmercifully in the rain. One squad occupied each square structure. The insides were covered with graffiti, including names, class dates, and missives of wisdom dating back to the beginning. For a "tabbed" Ranger, these weathered and worn structures project the elevated aura of a shrine.

Non-airborne students arrive by a "deuce-n-half," a 2-1/2-ton truck. Even without rank insignia, a pecking order will have developed, and the lowest man will find himself perched on the rucksacks piled on the truck's floor. These tired men quickly embrace the opportunity to sleep during the five-hour ride north. Sleep will soon be nothing but a dream.

Approximately 50 percent of the class that start the Benning Phase make it to the Mountain Phase in Dahlonega. Chances are that 90 percent of those completing

Ranger students practice belay techniques during the lower mountaineering training phase at Camp Merrill. Built on a steep slope, this platform tops a 20-foot wooden wall that the students rappel down.

(right) A "go" on previous tasks allows the student to progress to the 60-foot rappel down a 45° rock slope. The Mountain Phase instructors are posted at the top, bottom, and middle of the rappel to provide ongoing verbal instruction and support. The student on rappel leans backward and positions his body as if sitting in a chair. The left hand guides the rope while the right hand acts as a hand brake.

the Mountain Phase will graduate. The intensity increases in this phase. The ideal Ranger will rise above the physical duress and mental anguish to become a leader. A great leader is calm and confident in his ability to assess a situation and execute a decision. Instruction focuses on taking quick, decisive action. During this time, the warrior leader will emerge.

During the Mountain Phase, students receive five days of instruction on military mountaineering tasks that are divided into lower and upper mountaineering training. Lower mountaineering training lasts three days and begins with more lessons in knot- and rope-tying. Students use these skills while hauling equipment up mountains and forging streams. Rope bridges, which are used to move men and equipment, are installed, broken down, then remade in a new location, where the students will conduct the movements all over again. They learn about belays, anchor points, rope management, and the basic fundamentals of climbing and rappelling. Students first learn rappelling on a 30-foot wooden wall, then test their skills on the 60-foot, water-soaked, rocky cliff. They rappel with and without rucksacks. In the past, Rangers tied their "Swiss seats" (harnesses around the waist and legs) using 13-foot segments of rope. Now, a "rigger's belt" of black, nylon webbing with a friction-lock (Fastex) buckle is used.

Upper mountaineering training culminates with a two day exercise requiring the application of the skills learned during lower mountaineering training. Upper mountaineering takes place on Mount Yonah. By the fifth day of Mountain Phase, unseasoned students test

A line of Rangers prepares to descend the mountain by rappelling. Each man is hooked into a guide rope by a snaplink connected to a figure-eight on his rigger's belt. This rope is a safety precaution, and men must make the climb themselves.

(left) From the top of Mount Yonah, students can see Tennessee, North Carolina, and the downtown Atlanta skyline on a clear day. The Cherokee word "yanu," or "yonah," means "bear." Looking from a distance at the granite monolith from the south, the rock has the resemblance of a bear. These students belay others scaling up the rock face during the upper mountaineering phase.

During lower mountaineering training, roster # 101 hooks in and prepares to rappel the 30-foot cliff. The RI gives belay instructions to another student, but before roster # 101 descends, he will check his rigging. Failure to assemble it correctly will result in a "no go" at this station.

(left) Mealtime in Mountain Phase. In this situation, Rangers are given five minutes to eat, and then it is time to pack up everything. One student (front right) rehydrates his Meal Ready to Eat (MRE) with water from his canteen.

their mountaineering skills by completing a mandatory 200-foot night rappel. Each student must successfully complete all of the climbs in order to continue any further in Ranger School. During the two field training exercises (FTXs), Ranger students perform patrol missions that require the use of their newly acquired skills.

Ranger students remain in the training environment, but their instructors rotate in and out of the camps. At the RI changeover, a new group of RIs relieves the old one and announces the new chain of command by selecting a platoon leader from the group of students. At the patrol base after the mission's typically pre-dawn conclusion, the instructors conduct After Action Reviews, counsel students, and designate each patrol leader either a "go" or a "no go." The Ranger students must show accountability of equipment and personnel. Medical personnel check everyone's feet for injuries. The newly appointed patrol leaders are given their missions, and the planning stages begin. The remaining men have the opportunity to maintain their equipment and possibly eat, shower, or sleep.

The same types of missions conducted at Camp Darby are conducted at Camp Merrill. However, students find employing squad and platoon for combat patrol operations within the mountainous environment decidedly more intense. The trees create possible hazards, and the

In a field between the forested hills, the RI instructs his students about a prescribed movement to make contact with the "enemy" force. The RI talks about which men should go on a leader's reconnaissance patrol and what they should do. The students rest on a knee and listen attentively.

On a patrol in the Mountain Phase, the platoon's POW and search team examines an enemy element for sensitive documents and equipment.

mountains shrink open areas for landing or drop zones. Students further develop their ability to command and control a platoon-size patrol through planning, preparing, and executing a variety of combat patrol missions. Planning and preparing is critical. The student appointed as platoon leader receives the mission from the RI and begins the planning process: planning for security, infiltration, extraction, accountability, and execution of the mission. In the planning bay, the appointed platoon leader and assistant platoon leader draft the plan on a series of large chalkboards. They delegate members of the squad to

(right) The acting platoon leader and platoon sergeant discuss the method for destroying the enemy's consolidated equipment, such as weapons, radios, LCEs, on the objective. The platoon leader directs the platoon sergeant to pass the simulated demolition, or demo, to the fire team. Once the entire platoon reaches the objective, the fire team sets up the demo, and everyone clears out. The last man from the fire team to leave the objective shouts, "Fire in the hole," then ignites the demolition.

When in doubt, read the instructions. Every student has the Ranger Handbook, a manual that contains all the how-to information for conducting every military tactical and procedural operation. In its original form, the handbook is pocket-sized and softbound with a standard bookbinding that would not survive Ranger School. Students disassemble their handbook, laminate both sides of each page individually, and punch two holes along the top. Two circular metal snap rings keep the book together. Many choose to tie the handbook with 550-cord instead, as it is more tactical. Fine-point permanent markers write well on the laminated pages for note taking.

In a clearing in the North Georgia Mountains, a Ranger School student kneels and watches the treeline as he rehearses how to cross dangerous areas and how to react to enemy contact. Strapped to his back is the AT-4 anti-tank weapon system.

In the Mountain Phase at Camp Merrill, the assigned platoon leader and the platoon sergeant plan the mission and prepare the operation order together. In the planning bay, they draft the plan on large chalkboards for all of the students in the patrol to view. Writing the plan can take up to two hours to complete. The operation order states who will do what, when, and where, how it will be done, and with what weaponry. The operations order also includes a weather report, map, modes of transportation, and a packing list. Each Ranger's job during the mission is delineated. A contingency plan is written as well as the routes for infiltration, exfiltration, and escape and evade (E and E).

(above) The UH-60 Blackhawk helicopter leaves the landing zone (LZ) and the platoon in the open meadow so they can begin their mission. They will move by foot to the objective and back to the patrol base.

(left inset) Immediately upon exiting the Blackhawk, these platoon members pull security while the remaining team members exit and move into position. They wait for the helicopter to take off before joining the patrol.

A class of Ranger students has completed the first half of the Mountain Phase. They receive a block of instruction about entering and exiting the UH-60 Blackhawk aircraft.

make a terrain map or write and verbally "brief back" (return a report in summary) parts of the operations order.

At this point in training, the human desire for sleep is probably the most difficult to resist. The body will eventually enter some state of respite whether the human mind consciously wants it to or not. Unauthorized sleeping earns negative marks—sometimes thick, red, Sharpie marker lines across one's neck. This is not meant as a joke. The sleeping Ranger awakens to a "neck check," which signifies a throat slit by the enemy during sleep. Sleeping while pulling security is the worst violation, as it may allow the enemy to enter the patrol base and kill people without being detected. Some RIs may inscribe carefully chosen words across a dozing Ranger's forehead. In the absence of mirrors, a Ranger may bear these marks for some time before someone breaks the news.

A Ranger would gladly bear the shame of a scarlet Sharpie rather than encounter a worse consequence for

This student is signaling to the patrol that this is a "listening halt." Everyone must stop immediately and remain motionless and quiet for approximately 60 seconds. This is conducted to assure that there is no other movement nearby, such as someone following the patrol.

The platoon leader, holding the map, signals for the POW and search teams to fall out and find the enemy element. The patrol has already assaulted, or hit, the objective and reconsolidate as a unit. The POW and search teams look for enemy personnel, check the bodies, and search for sensitive documents they may have.

After assaulting across the objective, a Ranger School student awaits further orders from the platoon leader. He remains ready to respond and continues to scan the perimeter with a watchful eye. The mission is not complete until an aircraft at the LZ picks them up.

On a raid in the Mountain Phase, the cautious M240 Bravo gun team pulls security on a "likely avenue of approach," otherwise defined as the most likely way the enemy may enter the area. Students must be prepared for a possible counter-attack from a reactionary force or enemy personnel that has escaped from the recently assaulted objective.

sleeping: the loss of weapon. To avoid losing sensitive items, Rangers characteristically tie belongings to their bodies with 550-cord. However, an RI will sometimes cut the 550-cord and take a sleeping Ranger's weapon. Upon awaking, the student is hit with panic and punishment. On some occasions, an exhausted Ranger will awaken to find his weapon among a pile of others. The student must then report to the RI to retrieve his weapon and receive a negative major spot report.

The Ranger student continues to learn how to sustain himself and his men in the adverse conditions of the mountains. The rugged terrain and weather as well as the hunger, physical fatigue, and emotional stress that the student encounters allow him the opportunity to gauge his own capabilities and limitations. He also learns how to interpret his men's strengths and weaknesses as well as those of his Ranger buddy.

Within this training environment, Ranger students conduct combat patrol missions against a conventionally equipped, threatening force in a low-intensity, conflict scenario. These patrol missions occur day and night over a four-day squad FTX and a five-day platoon FTX. These

A SAW gunner provides security as the aid-and-litter team prepares to evacuate a "wounded" comrade using a plastic sled stretcher.

The body becomes so tired during Ranger School that the mind begins to play tricks. One Ranger student claims that if he stood somewhere long enough, he would see things that were not there and could not be there. Sometimes he felt his eyes were closed, yet he still had complete vision of the surroundings. "Droning" is the 1,000-yard, absent stare, as if one is mentally in a faraway land. Ranger buddies will talk about anything to keep each other awake. Some employ desperate measures such as dropping Tabasco sauce in their eyes to keep them open. Others use coffee grounds from MREs as snuff and try to benefit from the caffeine.

missions include ambushing the enemy force and mounting an attack by raiding and destroying a fixed installation. Ranger students reach their objectives in several ways: moving cross-country over mountains, conducting a river crossing, scaling steep slopes, marching 8 to 10 miles over the Tennessee Valley Divide, or landing air assaults from MH-60 Blackhawk helicopters into small landing zones on the sides of mountains. Ranger students must perform when they are tired, hungry, cold, wet, dirty, and stressed. The Ranger students are pushed to the limits of endurance. And then they are pushed again. Subsequently, they are given their missions and must lead physically expended and emotionally exhausted students to accomplish yet another combat patrol mission.

In this team effort, everyone must apply complete and unfaltering effort, no matter what the odds are of being successful. Lack of motivation hinders the mission. Rangers acquire personal knowledge of intestinal fortitude and learn to conquer the unthinkable.

Florida Phase

The 2nd Ranger Battalion, activated on April 1, 1943, was trained and led by Lieutenant Colonel James Earl Rudder. Rudder's men successfully carried out the most dangerous mission of the Omaha Beach landings in Normandy, France. On June 6, 1944, three companies of the 2nd Ranger Battalion, while under intense gunfire, assaulted the perpendicular cliffs of Point Du Hoc and

At the end of Mountain Phase, the 5th RTB chaplain holds nondenominational chapel services, which routinely receive an overwhelming response from the Ranger students. The services offer worshipers a chance to partake in Holy Communion, which is comprised of a slice of bread and grape Kool-Aid.

First priority is cleaning the weapons. Well-maintained and dependable equipment contributes to a mission's success.

destroyed a large gun battery that would have otherwise wreaked havoc on the Allied fleets offshore. For two days and nights, they fought without relief. The Florida Phase Ranger training camp is named after this heroic World War II commander who led the pivotal mission.

At the conclusion of the Mountain Phase, the students travel to the final phase. Those who are not airborne-qualified arrive by bus, while those with jump wings enter by parachute assault. By land or air, these hardened warriors wind up in the Florida Phase, conducted at Camp (James E.) Rudder, which is located near Eglin Air Force Base at Florida's Fort Walton Beach area. At this point, the Ranger class has spent countless hours training, rehearsing, and implementing knowledge imparted by the RIs. During this phase, instruction emphasizes the continuing development of the Ranger students' functional combat arms skills. There is focus on planning and leading platoon-size units on independent operations, and an emphasis on operations coordinated with airborne, air assault, small boat, and ship-to-shore operations. This is achieved through patrol operation exercises at the platoon level while in a swampy, jungle-like environment. The Florida Phase replicates a low-intensity combat environment against a well-trained, sophisticated enemy. It is here in the swamps that an opposing force is added, making the training more comparable to a combat situation. The Ranger students have progressed from the crawl phase at Benning and the walk phase of the mountains to the run phase of Florida.

The Florida Phase training for the jungle or swamp environment includes small-boat operations, ship-to-shore operations, and expedient stream-crossing techniques. The students are also taught survival skills. Out in the salty, blue Gulf of Mexico, squads of Rangers capsize and recapsize Zodiac boats. The students learn how to enter and exit the boat while in the water. They contend with the rolling surf and assault the shore by Zodiacs. Depending on the time of year and the tide elevations, the swamps and rivers further inland can become chest-deep. Fog can also become an obstacle. The Florida Phase has

During Florida Phase, classes are given on the reptiles and amphibians found in the swamps. Snakebite emergency first-aid procedures are taught as a precaution. Students have the opportunity to handle the nonpoisonous snakes of the southeastern United States. Poisonous snakes indigenous to this area include the eastern diamondback rattlesnake, water or cottonmouth moccasin, eastern coral snake, and copperheads. Nonvenomous king snakes constrict and engulf small prey. The snakes found in the 6th RTB's reptile house are extremely large—up to five feet long and as thick as a man's arm. The reptile house is home to the many reptiles and amphibians used by the 6th RTB for instructional purposes.

By the time Florida Phase arrives, the students are a cross between walking cadavers and sleep-deprived zombies. "If you stood somewhere long enough, you'd get tunnel vision, or begin to see things that really were not and could not be there," one Ranger School student explains. The body becomes so tired that the mind begins to play bizarre tricks. Some have sworn that their eyes were closed, yet they still had total vision of their surroundings.

An M-203 grenade launcher is strapped to the back of a student leaving the riverbank for a movement through the wet Florida forest.

implemented sophisticated water- and weather-monitoring systems. The waterways are carefully monitored for changing conditions, as Rangers conduct several stream crossings with a one-rope bridge. By squad and platoon, they paddle Zodiac boats through swamps and down rivers to the objective. Water operations leave the men salty and sandy, caked with mud and soaked to the skin.

The Ranger students are updated on the mission's scenario, and they band together as a platoon-size unit to complete the mission. The result is an extremely intense and utterly exhausting field training exercise of daytime and nighttime raids and ambushes through the dank, muggy, saturated swamp. The platoon begins with an airborne insertion, then proceeds across streams and through swamps. It accelerates the pace as the field training's 10-day exercise pushes students to the limits of endurance, both physical and emotional. The FTX culminates with a 16-kilometer (9.9-mile) forced road march.

With intestinal fortitude burning deep inside, the Ranger students will hopefully rise to the occasion and lead their subordinates on a successful mission. Students

Breaks in contact become more common. The Ranger file, or line of students, may move out for 40 meters while a "droning" student just stands there. Someone behind him in the file notices, and with a yell and a slap on the back of his PC, the file gets moving again. Hopefully, the students can link back up with the others. If not, the acting platoon sergeant or platoon leader for that patrol gets a "no-go" for failing to keep control of his elements. "Drones" stare as though they have mentally entered a land far, far away. These Florida Phase Ranger students are moving down a road to conduct water operations.

Before the students proceed into the Zodiacs and down the river, they receive a block of instruction from the RI. Safety precautions, such as wearing life vests, are sensible practices to guard the Rangers' lives. Capsizing drills are conducted in the event that the raft actually turns over during a mission. The Zodiac has lines that are attached for this very purpose. Each man in the squad has a designated numbered position on the boat. One person will stand up on the side while holding on to the rope and then lean back to capsize the boat. The challenging part is righting the boat and replacing all the men and equipment inside. Everything is tied down—with the exception of the soldiers themselves. It takes a greater amount of effort to right the boat, and sometimes a man is thrown through the air to splash down on the boat's opposite side.

with the intense desire for the elite Ranger designation will persevere, which motivates others to overcome pitfalls in the highly stressful, challenging situations they will now encounter. Upon completion of the Florida Phase of training, airborne-qualified students conduct an airborne insertion into Fort Benning, while the remaining students are trucked in.

The Ranger Course Pam-phlet states, "During the Ranger course, the Ranger proves he can overcome seemingly insurmountable mental and physical challenges. He

The river embankments make moving the Zodiacs in and out of the river an exhausting challenge. Here, the students load the rubber boat to conduct a movement down river.

(next pages) The RI must accompany the platoon on its patrol in order to grade the platoon leader and platoon sergeant. He is also present to ensure safe practices. Here, the RI is front and center on the boat to observe any possible changing river conditions.

has demonstrated, while under simulated combat conditions, that he has acquired the professional skills and techniques necessary to plan, organize, coordinate, and conduct small unit operations.

The student ahead of the others, known as the point man, leads the way. The patrol leader designates the best man to fill the point man position, as he is the navigator. The students quickly learn of each other's strengths and weaknesses, and a wise leader will organize his patrol accordingly.

He has demonstrated that he has mastered basic skills needed to plan and execute dismounted small-unit day and night operations, low-altitude mountaineering, and infiltration as well as exfiltration techniques via land, air, and sea. As a result of proving that he can successfully accomplish these tasks during the Ranger course, he is authorized to wear the Ranger Tab."

The exhausted and emaciated men welcome graduation day with pride and gratefulness. Many are in the worst physical shape of their lives, and it may take up to a year to regain the muscular mass, endurance, and strength with which they came to Ranger School. Uniforms hang loosely on the students' bodies as they march across Hurley Hill's field for the ceremony. "Rangers in Action," which precedes the actual ceremony, is an hour of demonstrations performed by the Ranger Training Brigade to impress the guests in attendance. Rangers "helo-cast," or drop from hovering helicopters, into Victory Pond. They fast-rope from the helicopters and demonstrate Special Patrol Insertion/Extraction System (SPIES) rigging, a system where men are fastened into rigging, then carried away on long cables by helicopter. "Rangers in Action" also showcases Victory Pond's slide-for-life, hand-to-hand combat, knife fighting, and drill marches. The crowd can see and hear about the weapons and capabilities of a Ranger squad during an equipment orientation. Mothers and fathers, sisters and brothers, wives, children, and friends wait for the "pinning of the Tab." Especially for those students from the Ranger Regimental Headquarters or one of the three Ranger Battalions, unit commanders often make the trip to watch their men graduate. Likewise, platoon or squad leaders

(left) A platoon contained in three Zodiacs moves down a Florida river. Summer months in Florida keep the swamps low and the heat index high. Patrol movements are limited to the distance from one water hole to the next. If a Ranger collapses from heat exhaustion, he is stripped of his equipment and submerged into the nearest water source. Ranger School medics move the overheated student to an aid station where he is popped with an IV and pumped with cherry Kool-Aid. Most do not want to spend too much time in the aid station. If a student misses more than 72 hours of training during the entire Ranger course, he is recycled or dropped.

In the Florida Phase, stress is increased by 100 percent because some of the students need a "go" on graded patrols to graduate. Tempers become testy, as seen on the face of the person leading the patrol.

(left) The "Rangers in Action" helocast from a hovering Blackhawk at Victory Pond during their demonstration at the Ranger School graduation. The bag contains rucksacks made into a poncho raft to be swam across the pond.

(right) It has been an exhausting and grueling eight weeks, and the lack of food and sleep has taken its toll. Their wide-open eyes contrast their hollowed cheeks as students complete their final patrol.

(below) The elite tab at last. A wife proudly pins the black and gold tab onto her husband. His uniform hangs on his body and appears a size too big. Graduates are awarded the black and gold tab on graduation day, which is later sewn on the Class A or dress uniform. The BDU tab is subdued in black and olive-green.

from the soldiers' units commonly attend. At the Ranger School graduation, awards are granted to recognize those with outstanding achievement during the Ranger Course. Depending on class performance, either all or just some of these awards will be presented, as no requirement demands that every award be issued for each graduating class.

For the students, this has been the longest two months of their lives. But it has also been an unforgettable experience that will last a lifetime.

The 75th Ranger Regiment is a flexible, highly trained, and rapidly deployable light-infantry force with specialized skills that enable it to be employed against a variety of conventional and special operations targets. The mission of the 75th Ranger Regiment is direct action (DA), meaning it plans and conducts special military operations in any operational environment. Rangers must be ready to deploy anywhere in the world given only an 18-hour notice. They are experts at infiltrating by land, sea, or air, into any kind of terrain, and under any type of condition.

The Rangers are the nation's premier strike force. Give a Ranger a mission, and it will be done correctly the first time and in a well-planned, well-rehearsed manner. He may arrive by parachuting from an airplane, fast-roping from a hovering helicopter, or jumping out the back of a transport. In some cases, the helicopter may hover only long enough for him to step off directly to the ground. The soldier will then be off and running. If the terrain prohibits running, the Ranger will swim, climb, crawl, rappel, hop, skip, or jump with speed. He will cross rivers, move through jungles, scale mountain cliffs, and assault beachfronts. This elite warrior will not be alone. His comrades will be there beside him, operating with the same expertise, intensity, and motivation. Both alone and as part of a team, soldiers will uphold the tenets of their Ranger Creed.

All Rangers are taught to execute raids, ambushes, and reconnaissance actions at both squad and platoon levels. These combat leaders are experts in patrolling and surviving. Not only do they master these skills, they also teach them to their subordinates. Rangers train year-round in various terrain, climates, and weather conditions. Training takes place day or night. The process of rehearsing tactics in the training environment allows Rangers to learn from and not repeat mistakes. They will rehearse a mission until it becomes instinctive. This process results in finely tuned operations with a strong record of success.

After Action Review (AAR) is an interactive process that provides immediate feedback on each element, from platoon

Masked by the deep vegetation, the SAW gunner comes up to a kneeling position to fire on enemy bunkers during a squad movement to contact lane. With Wiley-X eye protection, communications, and an on-the-move hydration system, this Ranger supports a team as it moves forward to take the objective.

through brigade task force. The procedure takes place immediately after the mission, be that in the jungle, by a stream, in the woods, or along the drop zone. The commander or leader conducting the AAR positions himself where he can be seen and heard, and the Rangers gather around him. The commander states what was right and what was wrong, and offers solutions to problems. Each man has an opportunity to talk about his mission, what he saw and did, and how he solved problems that arose during the mission. The AAR's impartial feedback encourages interaction and discussion by all members of the unit. Every AAR explores the unit's strengths and weaknesses, identifies its good and bad trends, and provides an opportunity to determine how its weaknesses will be fixed and by whom.

strategic targets in order to better secure the area. Once the "follow up" forces arrive, the Rangers move on out.

The 75th Ranger Regiment offers unprecedented opportunities for professional growth, development, and promotion. In addition to infantry specialties, the 75th Ranger Regiment needs soldiers who have skills in fields ranging from communication and culinary arts to medical and mechanical expertise.

Soldiers who thrived on the rigors of Basic Training and the thrills of Airborne School, yet hunger for more challenge and adventure, generally choose to be Rangers. Out of all the army's regular and special operations units, the Ranger Regiment routinely employs the most intense and grueling physical training regimen. The Ranger Regiment is the only unit that mandates physical training five days a week, 48 weeks a year. Rangers are allotted more training time and financial resources than other units as well as overseas deployment and off-post training opportunities. They use state-of-the-art equipment and cutting-edge technological systems. Selection rates for promotion, schooling, and command positions are higher than the army averages. Ranger units have the highest percentage of NCOs who later become officers in the army. Last, soldiers have the personal and professional satisfaction of contributing to the finest and most elite regiment in the U.S. Army.

Although the U.S. Army provides today's Rangers technologically advanced equipment and weapon systems, cutting-edge technology is no substitute for knowledge, ingenuity, and common sense. Rangers train with advanced equipment systems as well as the old-fashioned methods. Outside of Ranger life, malfunctioning or broken equipment can delay or even cancel activities. In the Rangers, such excuses don't exist. Rangers complete the mission regardless of equipment failure. For example, Rangers can build a fully functioning 2992 antenna with wire, 550-cord,

The Bravo Company, 1st Ranger Battalion commander leads an AAR while the Rangers are on the objective. The squad listens intently so mistakes and poor practices will not be repeated. The squad then has the opportunity to attack the position again.

Ranger missions may include target demolition, deep penetration raids, and precision ambushes. Recovery or rescue operations for personnel and equipment are possible Ranger missions. Rangers may also conduct reconnaissance operations of a shortened duration, usually limited to three days. A mission of such shortened duration would not require resupply. A typical Ranger mission might be seizing an airfield for use by general-purpose forces that are already in transport or conducting raids on key operational and

and poles found in the area and can do so from scratch in little time. Rangers learn range estimation skills to determine distance without the use of binoculars equipped with an electronic range-finder feature. Rangers can use calculators, but in the event of equipment failure or loss, they are able apply basic math skills to make computations. Land navigation is made easier with a Global Positioning System (GPS); however, Rangers learn the triangulation method of using a compass, a method based on known points, azimuths, and points of intersection. The resourceful Ranger, having been trained that there is more than one way to do almost anything, even knows how to use pieces of fencing found in the field to make a Bangalore torpedo.

All Ranger Battalions are organized in an identical manner. Each has three rifle or combat companies, a battalion headquarters company, and a headquarters company. The U.S. Army authorizes a Ranger Battalion 580 men with up to

(below) A Ranger communicates to the company medics that more casualties were taken on and more men were needed to extract the bodies to the casualty collection point. Rangers rehearse every possible scenario in training exercises to better prepare them for real-world situations.

(above) A Ranger private talks about his responsibilities and actions as he took the objective with his squad. An AAR can take as long as an hour. The practical application of skills in training exercises coupled with immediate feedback and correction drastically enhances the "cherries'" acquisition of new skills.

15 percent over-staffing due to TDY and attending schools. According to 2001 statistics, the Ranger Regiment had an estimated 2,300 men. In the future, class size is expected to grow, as evidenced by a recent RIP class that enrolled 575 men, the largest RIP class in Ranger history.

The battalion headquarters company includes the company's headquarters, the fire support team, the medical team, and the communications team. There is also a support section, which includes food services.

The rifle companies consist of approximately 150 Rangers each, with the remaining men in the Ranger Battalion assigned to the headquarters company. A rifle company is comprised of three rifle platoons of about 45 men each and a weapons platoon of 20 or so men. Members of the rifle squads take lightweight, automatic weapons with them on an assault. Squad medics also carry rifles. The weapons platoon contains three sections: a mortar section, an anti-tank section, and a sniper section. The mortar section has two 60-millimeter mortars with a third available for special operations. The anti-tank section is supplied with three three-man teams that are assigned to the 84-millimeter Ranger Anti-tank Weapon System (RAWS). The weapons platoon

Medical personnel assess the Priority of Movement, as the most seriously wounded are extracted first. An IV and bandages are applied as initial first- aid measures. Medics are able to provide first-aid for cuts and open wounds, head trauma, broken bones, burns, shock, and spinal and neck injuries. Each Ranger Battalion is allotted a battalion surgeon, a highly qualified and extensively experienced medic who can perform emergency surgery on the battlefield if necessary.

Rangers are experts in land navigation and in patrolling behind enemy lines. A "plugger" system can pinpoint the squad's location within one meter and transfer the locale information to the chain of command. In the patrol base, the squad leader checks the map as the men begin with Priorities of Work.

also has two two-man sniper teams armed with the M24 and a third two-man team armed with the .50-caliber Barrett Sniper System.

Each Ranger Battalion has a Ranger Support Element that operates in support of the Ranger's training at their home station. The support element does not deploy with the Ranger Battalion. Instead, this unit of parachute riggers, truck drivers, maintenance workers, and the like operates from their home station and provides the battalion with all the necessary services to meet training and deployment demands.

Firepower is essential, and available resources and equipment are consistent among the Ranger Battalions. Each battalion is allotted these weapon systems as a standard: 84-millimeter RAWS, 60-millimeter mortars, M240G machine guns, MK19 grenade launchers, .50-caliber machine guns, Javelins, and M249 Squad Automatic Weapons.

A modified Land Rover called a Ranger Special Operations Vehicle (RSOV) carries a six- to seven-man crew. Each Ranger Battalion possesses twelve of these specialized vehicles. The main purpose of the RSOV is to provide the Rangers with mobile defense capability. It is not an assault vehicle, but it is useful in establishing battle positions that provide the force some standoff capability for a short duration, such as during an airfield seizure mission. The RSOV mounts an M240G machine gun and either an MK19 grenade launcher or M2 .50-caliber

A Ranger squad leader commands the squad to breach a wire obstacle leading to the objective. Rangers use explosives, wire cutters, or even a buddy's body to breach the wire. Speed is essential because the enemy likely has weapons fixed on the possible locations of entry. Anything slowing the Rangers makes them the enemy's target.

To breach the wire, 1st Battalion Rangers fire onto bunkers as the squad bounds forward. The Ranger squad leader controls the men from the center. Once contact is made with the objective, he usually moves closely behind the assault element while always remaining in contact with the support element.

machine gun. One passenger operates an anti-armor weapon such as the RAWS, Javelin, Light Anti-tank Weapon (LAW), or AT-4.

RSOV platoons are also equipped with a number of military motorcycles. From 1988 to 1995, the Rangers relied on the Honda CR250. In 1996, they switched to the Kawasaki KLR250, which is still used today, along with a newer bike, which is based on the Suzuki DS80. One of the more useful features of this smaller bike is that it can be palletized more easily and dropped from aircraft along with the Rangers.

The 84-millimeter RAWS is also referred to as the Carl Gustav. This weapon is unique to the Ranger Battalions and is not currently being tested or used by other infantry units. This versatile weapon is a "crew-served" weapon, meaning that it takes a two-man team, the gunner and assistant gunner, to operate it effectively. It can fire high-explosive (HE) and high-explosive anti-tank (HEAT) rounds, illumination rounds, and smoke rounds. The weapon's effective range varies with its type of ammunition. In the future, it will be able to fire an 84-millimeter, highly destructive, flechette (pages 100-101) Rangers from 1st Battalion must exert enormous effort in order to secure an objective during a live-fire raid exercise at Fort Stewart, Georgia. Rangers are known to move faster and fight harder than any other types of soldiers. Speed yields surprise. When not moving the wounded, the Skedco stretcher (seen on the back of the soldier on the left) can be used to drag important pieces of equipment from the objective area.

Sometimes one just sits and waits. A Ranger waits to move the RSOV to Hunter Army Airfield. This specifically modified Land Rover is an off-road vehicle with all of the essential tools on board: spiked tire cutters, shovels, wire cutters, water, fuel, stretcher, and .50-caliber machine gun.

The RSOV from 2nd Ranger Battalion sits poised and ready for action. The likelihood of these wide wheel-based, all-terrain vehicles rolling is minimal. Green Beret units have adapted a similar vehicle with a flat steel platform in place of the roof. This allows special forces soldiers to enter a building directly onto the second story.

Ranger Special Operations Vehicles (RSOVs) and motorcycles are used to secure an airfield or roadway intersection that leads to the objective area. These Kawasaki 250s can transport two riders and have infrared capabilities. A Ranger's weapon is placed across the handlebars on a specifically designed rack.

round. Currently it is designed to combat concrete bunkers, heavy armor, armored personnel carriers, and aircraft. A three-man crew fires one of the sixteen RAWSs in each Ranger Battalion.

The M224 fires mortar rounds that are 60 millimeters in diameter. This weapon's purpose is to provide the company commander with indirect fire, and its relatively lighter weight of 46-1/2 pounds makes it well-suited for light infantry and special operations units, such as the Rangers. It is a muzzle-loaded weapon that can be drop-fired or trigger-fired. It is either fired while mounted on a base plate on the ground or from the hand-held position The M224 features

a spring shock absorber to absorb the shock of recoiling when firing. The gun's mechanisms can elevate and position the mortar, making it a high-angle-of-fire weapon. The four 60-millimeter mortars in each battalion are crew-served weapons. Additional mortars are found in each Ranger Battalion. The M29A1 and M259 versions of the 81-millimeter mortar are additional crew-served, indirect-fire weapons that offer maximum effective range of 5,700 meters. This 81-millimeter mortar weighs just under 90 pounds. The M120 and M121 are heavy mortars with a 120-millimeter round. These weapons provide a high-angle of fire and are used to support ground troops. Weighing in at

nearly 320 pounds each, they are transported on an RSOV that is specifically rigged for the heavy mortar.

The M240G medium-class machine gun fires standard NATO 7.62-millimeter ammunition and is used as a support fire. It is a crew-served weapon. It has a removable barrel that can be changed easily to prevent overheating. The weapon has an integral, folding bipod and can also be mounted on a folding tripod for greater stability. When mounted, its maximum effective range is 1.8 kilometers (1.1 miles). This machine gun has a cyclic rate of fire between 650 and 950 rounds per minute, depending on the regulator setting. Each Ranger Battalion is allotted 27 of these machine guns.

The M249 Squad Automatic Weapon System (SAWS) is a light machine gun capable of delivering a large volume of effective fire to support infantry squad operations with accuracy similar to a rifle. It is a gas-operated, disintegrating, metallic-link, belt-fed weapon that fires standard NATO 5.56-millimeter ammunition. Although a 200-round disintegrating belt is standard, it can also fire a 20- or 30-round M16-series rifle's magazine. Its maximum effective range is 1,000 meters (about 1,094 yards). An individual can carry this weapon, as it weighs approximately 15 pounds. A gunner's basic load of 600 rounds of linked ammunition weighs a little more than 20 pounds. The SAWSs' cyclic rate of 725 rounds per minute provides the basis of firepower for the rifle team. Each Ranger Battalion is provided with 54 of these weapons.

The MK19, or Mark-19, grenade machine gun can fire a variety of 40-millimeter grenades at a rate of over 350 grenades per minute with a maximum range of over 2,200 meters (2,400 yards). The grenade launcher along with its cradle and tripod weighs about 137 pounds and is usually found mounted to Ranger Special Operations Vehicles. Each Ranger Battalion is allotted 12 of these grenade launchers. The 40-millimeter grenade can pierce armor up to two inches thick and can produce fragments that can kill personnel within 5 meters (16.4 feet) of the point of impact and wound personnel within 15 meters (49.2 feet) of the point of impact.

The Browning M2 .50-caliber machine gun is an automatic, belt-fed, crew-served weapon. The 128-pound gun

The large and powerful MH47 Chinook helicopter carries special operations vehicles like Zodiacs, RSOVs, and motorcycles. Rangers disembark from the helicopter and race to their assigned blocking positions to stop reactionary forces or enemy reinforcements that may attempt to enter the conflict. After the mission exercise is accomplished, the MH-47 will land to pick up the RSOV, motorbikes, "wounded," and "prisoners."

In support of a live-fire raid, the 1st Battalion 60-millimeter mortar team puts a round down range. Precise coordination with special operations air assets is conducted and monitored to avoid any unwanted contact. After the mortars deliver their rounds, the AH-6J Little Birds swoop in with gun and rocket runs.

The 2nd Battalion Rangers fire on hard targets with an 81-millimeter Carl Gustav weapon system during a live-fire training exercise at Fort Lewis, Washington.

Before the raid begins, the 3rd Battalion Ranger mortars section readies itself and waits for its fire mission. If the enemy compromises the support element or assault elements, the mortars will kick into action and provide indirect cover fire with 60-, 81-, and 120-millimeter ammunition.

and tripod are crew-transportable with limited amounts of ammunition for short distances, but carrying such a heavy weapon system is usually not the preferred method of transport. The Ranger Battalion more frequently mounts the M2 on its RSOV as an anti-personnel or anti-aircraft weapon, which yields a maximum effective range of 2,000 meters (about 2,200 yards). The M2 provides suppressive fire for offensive and defensive purposes, and can be used effectively against light-armored vehicles, low- and slow-flying aircraft, personnel, and small boats. Twelve M2 machine guns are supplied per Ranger Battalion.

These hefty, 60-millimeter mortars are placed on a rucksack in preparation for a live-fire exercise.

(left) Rangers from the 2nd Battalion answer the call for fire on "enemy troops" in the open. The 60-millimeter mortars can fire on fixed or moving targets. Rangers can fire this mortar system from a moving, rubber Zodiac boat by lining the floor with sheets of wood, covering it with sandbags, and placing the mortar on top.

A 2nd Ranger Battalion M240G gun team provides cover fire as members of its platoon attack a bunker complex at Fort Lewis, Washington.

The Javelin and Stinger are two shoulder-fired, portable guided missile weapons designed to engage tracked, wheeled, or amphibious vehicles as well as low-altitude jets, helicopters, unmanned aerial vehicles, and cruise missiles. Each of the systems is a "fire and forget" weapon, which aids in keeping the Ranger's load light. At a minimum, each Ranger Battalion keeps nine Javelin weapon systems. The LAW from the M72-series weaponry and the AT-4 are other lightweight, shoulder-fired, anti-armor weapons employed by the Rangers.

The Colt M4 Carbine is the compact version of the M16A2 rifle and is the replacement rifle for the M16-series rifle and other selected weaponry. The M4 Carbine is a lightweight, gas-operated, air-cooled, magazine-fed machine gun. It fires standard NATO 5.56-millimeter ammunition. This weapon is fired from the shoulder and has a collapsible stock. The use of a selector lever gives the soldier the option of either automatic fire (three-round bursts) or semi-automatic fire (single shot). The M4 allows soldiers operating within close quarters the capability to engage targets at extended range with accurate, lethal fire. For combat in close quarters, the M4 can be fitted with the M68 sight. The M68 sight is a reflex, or nontelescopic, sight. It uses a red, aiming reference, or collimated dot, and is designated for the "two eyes open" method of sighting. This method allows for quick acquisition of the target with a high probability of engaging the target. The M7 bayonet-knife is used as a bayonet on the M4 carbine and as a hand weapon.

RANGER CREED

Recognizing that I volunteered as a Ranger, fully knowing the hazards of my chosen profession, I will always endeavor to uphold the prestige, honor, and high esprit de corps of my Ranger Regiment.

Acknowledging the fact that a Ranger is a more elite soldier who arrives at the cutting edge of battle by land, sea, or air, I accept the fact that, as a Ranger, my country expects me to move further, faster, and fight harder than any other soldier.

Never shall I fail my comrades. I will always keep myself mentally alert, physically strong, and morally straight, and I will shoulder more than my share of the task, whatever it may be, one hundred percent and then some.

Gallantly will I show the world that I am a specially selected and well trained soldier. My courtesy to superior officers, neatness of dress, and care of equipment shall set the example for others to follow.

Energetically will I meet the enemies of my country. I shall defeat them on the field of battle for I am better trained and will fight with all my might. Surrender is not a Ranger word. I will never leave a fallen comrade to fall into the hands of the enemy and under no circumstances will I ever embarrass my country.

Readily will I display the intestinal fortitude required to fight on to the Ranger objective and complete the mission, though I be the lone survivor.

RANGERS LEAD THE WAY!

The Baretta M9 Personal Defense Weapon is a semi-automatic, double-action pistol with 9-millimeter ammunition. The M9 is carried by crew-served weapon crewmen, such as the M240G gunner and assistant gunner. The M9 is more lethal and lighter in weight than its predecessors. This compact pistol weighs only 2-1/2 pounds when fully loaded with its 15-round magazine. Its maximum effective range is 50 meters (about 164 feet).

Claymore mines and Bangalore torpedoes are explosives that have remained relatively constant in their design for decades. Today's M18A1 Claymore mine is packaged in a slightly bowed, cigar-box shaped container with C-4 explosive and approximately 700 small, steel balls. Its effective range is 50 meters (about 164 feet). Although Bangelore torpedoes are available in a kit, Rangers may improvise with a more "homemade" arrangement. Sections of fencing, wooden planks, or fence pickets are packed with C-4, wrapped with 100-mile-per-hour tape or secured with flex cuffs, and detonated with a blasting cap. Such explosives can clear a lane 1 meter (3.3 feet) in width, allowing Rangers to, for example, breach a barbed wire obstacle. Bangelores can also be used to clear minefields.

During water operations, the Rangers can paddle or mount an engine to the rear of a Zodiac landing craft for amphibious assaults. This rubber boat is ideal for Ranger special operations. It has flattened hulls and shallow drafts, which allow for greater accessibility through shallow rivers, waterways, low wetlands, and swampy areas. The Zodiac's design also

The assistant gunner of the M240G team feeds 7.62-millimeter ammunition into the machine gun. He is also responsible for adjusting the rounds on target by giving corrections in meters. After a large volume of fire is put through this machine gun, the barrel becomes extremely hot and can cause damage to the weapon. The assistant gunner is responsible for keeping the spare barrel and for changing barrels when appropriate. He also carries necessary night-vision equipment.

(opposite) "He's up. He sees me. I'm down," are the quick thoughts racing through a Ranger's mind in those three to five seconds that he is under enemy fire. Bravo Company, 1st Battalion's SAW gunner moves to his next position. Once he is there, the selection switch is turned to "fire," and the rest of his fire team moves under his cover fire.

The M249 SAW gunner scans his sector of fire for targets of opportunity. He knows his area of limitations to the right as his squad members are moving out to clear the other bunkers. He remains in position to cover the squad's advance toward the objective.

permits landing at sites not accessible to conventional boats such as beaches, riverbanks, marshes, and coral reef flats. Another feature that makes this craft especially useful for Rangers is its set of six air-filled compartments. The compartments are connected by valves, which allow the internal air pressure to be regulated. Therefore, the Zodiac will float even if one or more compartments becomes deflated. These specialized air compartments have the weight-carrying abilities to support a squad of Rangers and their equipment. When necessary, several Rangers can grab the carrying handles and portage the craft for limited distances.

The Ranger Battalion is outfitted with its own support element, transportation, and weaponry, chosen with regards to the necessary specialized operational requirements to accomplish the mission. The clothing and individual equipment provided for each Ranger is specialized in many ways as well. The standard infantry Personnel Armor System Ground Troops (PASGT) helmet is a one-piece construction made of multiple layers of Kevlar 29 fabric. The helmet provides ballistic protection for the head, neck, temple, and ear. The helmet adapted for the Ranger and airborne units includes the Parachutists' Impact Liner (PIL), a thick foam pad that provides impact protection, and a specialized chin-strap that helps maintain the helmet in position during airborne operations. The helmet weighs about three pounds.

A squad leader from the 3rd Ranger Battalion directs this M203 grenade launcher gunner to change his sector of fire. When Rangers reconsolidate after assaulting across the objective, they are always given sectors of fire to cover. This action holds back any kind of counterattack by the enemy. Interlocking sectors of fire can ward off almost any attack.

At Fort Pickett, Virginia, Rangers from 3rd Battalion load ammunition cans with .50-caliber rounds, then place their lot in the RSOV. Before the day is over, they will fire over 100,000 rounds of live ammunition. Repetitive training and frequent practice increase the likelihood of success on the battlefield.

The Kevlar PASGT vest, also referred to as a flak jacket, does not meet the Ranger's needs quite like the Ranger Body Armor (RBA) does. The RBA is specifically designed, ballistic body protection consisting of a flexible vest and a rigid plate. The flexible vest has a Kevlar filler with a camouflage nylon fabric exterior that can protect the front and back torso from most 9-millimeter rounds. It weighs approximately 8 pounds and is much lighter in weight than the approximately 25-pound flak jacket. When inserted into the front pocket of the vest, the 8-pound, rigid Ceramic Upgrade Plate provides additional front torso coverage. Its aluminum oxide, ceramic construction of 2x2-inch tiles protects an approximate 10x12-inch area from 5.56-millimeter and 7.62-millimeter rounds. The insert can be removed quickly and easily when it is not needed. An optional over-vest can be worn with the Ranger Body Armor to provide the back torso additional protection against small arms and flechette rounds. For the Ranger already protected by the rigid plate, this 16-1/2-pound Interim Small Arms Protective Over-vest would add additional protection to the back.

One of the Ranger's greatest weapons is the element of surprise, which is the advantage of night missions. Therefore, night vision is essential, and the lightweight AN/PVS-7D night-vision goggles are the state-of-the-art equipment used to meet this need. The night-vision goggles, commonly referred to by Rangers as "nods," are worn on the

An M203 mounted under an M4A1 rifle with a PSQ-4 sighting device aims to hit a small bunker port hole about 45 yards away. The luminous tape on the sighting device allows the weapon to be used during hours of limited visibility.

Hundreds of rounds of 7.62-millimeter ammunition spill out of the M240G weapon. A 3rd Battalion gunner checks his sector of fire prior to a raid. As part of the support element, this gun team waits for the signal to pour on the firepower.

head and over the face, and are held in place by head straps. The straps allow for one-handed mounting and dismounting. A binocular eyepiece assembly incorporates an infrared light source and amplifies existing ambient light to provide illumination and greater visibility during night operations. It is designed to work in conjunction with rifle-mounted aiming sights. It provides an optimal viewing distance of 150 to 350 meters (about 500 to 1,100 feet) and a focusing range of 25 centimeters (about 10 inches) to infinity. Its field of view is 40°. The nods operate for up to 50 hours on two AA alkaline batteries and weigh in at only 1-1/2 pounds.

The AN/PRC-119 radio is composed of a receiver and a transmitter. The radio has approximately 2,320 channels and includes voice and digital communication. The operating voltage for the radio is 13.5 volts from the primary battery. When on high power, it has a range of 5 to 10 kilometers (3.1 to 6.2 miles). The factors that affect the range are line of sight, location, weather, and surrounding noise level. The AN/PRC-126 radio is more lightweight than the 119 and is best used for squad operations. The radio-telephone operator in the squad or platoon frequently carries these portable radios. Today's Ranger is equipped with a small and lightweight individual radio, an ear-piece and microphone, and a control that straps to the wrist. By utilizing these items, the Ranger can avoid the hassle of having to pull the radio from a rucksack during intense operations.

Rangers carry with them all of their equipment, supplies, and provisions required for the mission, as resupply is highly unlikely. To aid with this, Rangers are issued the Modular Lightweight Load-carrying Equipment (MOLLE) System.

Boat movements down the Nisqually River near Tacoma, Washington, are tactically stealthful without outboard motors, but paddling makes for some long hours. These 2nd Battalion Rangers paddle downstream to link up with another Ranger element to conduct an ambush.

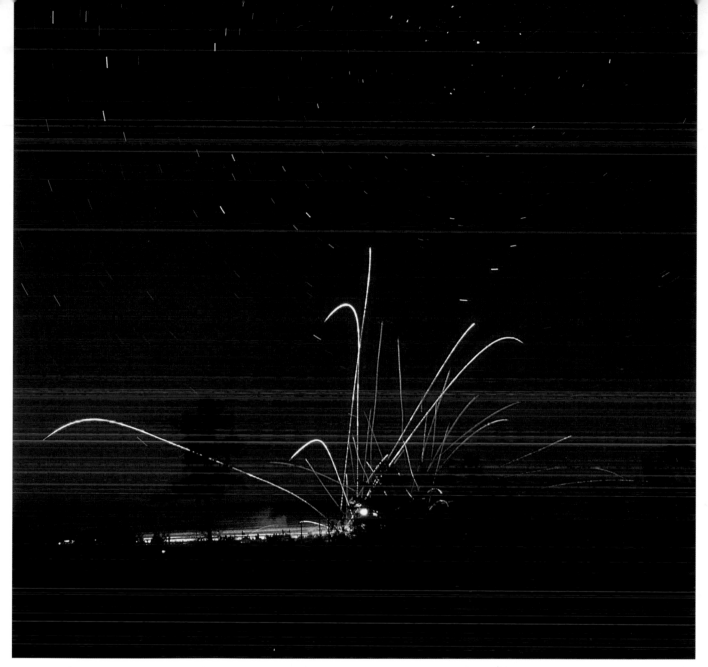

Rangers swiftly move onto the objective during a raid. Tracers light up the night sky so bright that, for a while, the stars cannot be seen. The support element pours fire power on the objective until signaled to "lift and shift" off those targets so the assault element can remove them altogether. Sixty-millimeter mortars, Little Birds, and AC-130 gunships prepare the objective prior to the Rangers setting foot in the objective's area of operation.

Portions of this pack can be removed if they are not needed, which allows soldiers to both adapt the pack for a variety of uses and reduce the weight of the pack itself. To a Ranger, this glorified backpack is called a "ruck" or "rucksack." Alone, it weighs almost 17 pounds. Once the Ranger is geared up, his weapon and equipment can weigh anywhere from 70 to 100 pounds. One popular portion of the MOLLE system is a "buttpack," or "fannypack," a pouch that straps around the waist and rides in the small of the back. It can carry approximately three days' worth of provisions and basic supplies. Fitting over the RBA is an assault vest Rangers can wear in place of the old and familiar Load-Carrying Equipment (LCE). The LCE has two padded suspender straps with an attached webbed waist belt. Just about anything imaginable can

be secured to the LCE with a clip or 550-cord. Rangers completely customize this apparatus according to their mission or assigned job.

The rucksack includes an on-the-move hydration system, a backpack-style water bladder with a self-sealing drinking tube. The most common manufacturer of this system is CamelBak, and Rangers have readily adopted the name in reference to this canteen substitute. Depending on the mission, combat soldiers usually carry 4 to 6 quarts of water in the field—that translates to two 1-quart canteens and one or more 2-quart canteens. These canteens are mounted on each hip in snap pouches, on the rucksack, or carried inside. This hydration system has a 2- to 3-liter insulated plastic pouch with a long, flexible straw that fits over the Ranger's shoulder and clips to the front, allowing him to drink whenever needed. It is possible to carry a 100-ounce pouch in the rucksack, another 100-ounce pouch in the attached patrol pack, and a 70-ounce pouch on the back, the combination of these totaling about 8 liters of water. The on-the-move hydration system permits the Ranger to keep his hands on his weapon and his eyes focused on the objective. He can drink easily during physical activity, road marches, or long movements. The human body can lose more than one liter of water per hour during intense physical activity. If water is not replaced, one can suffer heat stress, headaches, nausea, fatigue, and even temporary loss of muscle endurance and short-term memory.

The Ghillie Suit Accessory Kit (GSAK) items are packed in a flyer's kit bag and assembled by the snipers and long-range surveillance personnel when they attend their respective training courses. These kits also provide Rangers with the various camouflage components to construct, repair, and modify Ghillie Suits in order to meet unique mission and cli-

matic requirements. Soldiers will custom make each suit to their own specific designs and performance requirements. The kit consists of jute burlap strips in four colors; duck cloth; nylon cord; sewing needles and thread; foam padding; tie straps; white trousers, mittens, and parka for Arctic or snowy environments; camouflage face paint, netting, and covers; and several other accessory items. Natural colors, patterns, and textures that replicate the landscape's indigenous qualities are incorporated into the materials. To enhance the

In a Ranger Battalion, there seems to be a formation for everything. One Ranger recalls "hydration formations" during the hot weather months and during the days prior to training deployments in hot climates. The men were required to stand in formation in the common area and drink one two-quart canteen of water straight down. After a few minutes and on command, each Ranger would hold the canteen upside down over his head. To remain dry, he had to drink all of the water. No one was dismissed until all of the water was gone.

(above) Preparing to move out, the squad leader gives the command to "lock and load" as they progress down the movement to contact lane for a blank-fire exercise. Each Ranger has an individual communications device neatly tucked away in the MICH helmet, enabling contact with the team leader, squad leader, and platoon leader.

Following a long movement, a Ranger patrol sets into a patrol base hidden in the deep brush. Weapons maintenance is conducted on a rotation basis, cleaning and checking weapons a few at a time while keeping the rest ready. Weapons maintenance is not performed at night.

A Ranger from the 3rd Ranger Battalion wears night-vision goggles (NVG), which illuminate any available ambient light for improved vision in darkness. This Mark-19 40-millimeter grenade launcher is mounted to an RSOV.

dimensionality of the camouflage ensemble and break up the outline of his body, a Ranger sniper will cover his arms, back, and helmet with the natural vegetation. It is not uncommon for a Ranger to attach clumps of brush, twigs, leaves, or plants to himself as part of the camouflage process, as not every Ranger is afforded a GSAK.

Come rain or come shine, a Ranger is out in the weather. A lightweight rainsuit of GORE-TEX is the standard protection from the wind and rain. The waterproof parka has a drawstring hood and double front closure. The trousers have a drawstring waist and adjustable elastic ankle cuffs. Both parka and trousers stuff compactly into their own pockets.

The world famous Ka-Bar combat fighting survival knife with a fixed, 7-inch blade dates back to the World War II soldier. Many members of the U.S. Armed Services still depend

A Ranger talks about his training experiences in the jungles of Honduras. Everyone was briefed about the dangerous and poisonous creatures that could ruin a Ranger's day, or do even worse. This included highly poisonous, neon-colored frogs that supposedly possessed enough poison to kill 40 grown men. Such a threat leaves everyone walking on eggshells. At a listening halt, the Ranger and his assistant gunner (back in the days of the M60 machine gun) faced the machine gun to the file's rear across a fallen log. As they lay there, a neon frog innocently hopped along the downed tree. It was no bigger than a mouse. The two men stared at one another in astonishment, disbelieving that such a tiny creature could evoke such chilling fear. Afraid that the amphibian would jump at his jugular any moment, the Ranger withdrew his Ka-Bar and thrust it downward into the frog, pinning it to the log. It must have been a Ranger-qualified frog with a definite mission, because it continued to jump and hit the top of the Ka-Bar's handle, although it did not progress anywhere. The frog was a tough little thing. Finally, it was time to move out, so the Ranger removed the Ka-Bar from the log and the frog. The bright-neon frog continued hopping down the log to complete its mission.

(above) These 2nd Battalion Rangers secure their rucksacks in preparation for a raid. Movement through the deep woods affords good concealment for the camouflaged Rangers. The wet conditions absorb and soften the potential level of noise.

(left) On a patrol, a squad leader pinpoints the squad's location and identifies the routes, rally points, and suspected enemy locations on the map. A Global Positioning System (GPS) can accurately identify the patrol's location and can also coordinate indirect fire to come in dangerously close to its position while reducing the risk of getting hit.

on this basic weapon. The Leatherman-type, compact, multipurpose tool is another piece of equipment on which many Rangers depend. Made of stainless steel, this tool requires minimal maintenance to prevent rust and corrosion. Its design is a flat square or rectangle with tools neatly and cleverly tucked inside. This lends immediate access to knives, pliers, wire cutters, Phillips and flat screwdrivers, a bottle/can opener, scissors, and a fingernail file.

The resources available to the 75th Ranger Regiment go beyond gear and weaponry, and the Rangers are more than just men who can jump out of an airplane. The Regiment relies on Rangers who have specialties, or Military Occupational Specialties (MOSs), in a variety of areas. For example, the Rangers rely on 97B Counterintelligence Agents to ensure that the information on their capabilities, missions, and assets remains in the hands of right people. A communications specialist (MOS 31C, 31U, 31W, or 31Z) in the 75th Ranger Regiment specializes in state-of-the-art communications equipment. The Ranger Regiment's potential for worldwide

(above) As Rangers prepare to pull off the objective, medics and headquarters personnel ready the wounded for extraction and medical transport. This medic pulls a wounded Ranger on a Skedco stretcher. This pliable and durable plastic stretcher becomes rigid when the injured is secured inside. Attachable straps and handles allow for pulling along the ground, horizontal hoisting by helicopter, or vertical hoisting in confined spaces. Weighing less than 20 pounds, the stretcher compactly stores in a large pack. The platoon sergeant and first sergeant position themselves at the tail end of the helicopter's ramp to count personnel and maintain accountability of every Ranger. No one is left behind.

A 3rd Battalion Ranger medic checks the pulse on a wounded Ranger. An IV is started as the other Rangers continue the mission. During training such as this, Ranger leaders may assign men to act as casualties in order to enhance the realism. The medics must respond appropriately and perform care promptly, despite the mission raging on all around. The Ranger medic is one of the most highly trained and respected individuals in the Ranger Regiment.

Each Ranger Battalion is assigned a different shape of "cat eyes" for the backs of their patrol caps and rucksacks. The pieces of luminous tape glow much like a cat's eyes at night, which enables a Ranger to identify a fellow Ranger's location and even the battalion and company to which he is assigned. The cat eyes here are from Charlie Company, 1st Ranger Battalion.

assignments and the underlying possibility of nuclear, biological, and chemical warfare dictates the need for the technical and tactical skills of a 54B Chemical Specialist. The chemical specialist provides training regarding the proper use and maintenance of nuclear, biological, and chemical (NBC) detection and decontamination equipment. This specialist also performs NBC reconnaissance in the field and provides the Rangers with NBC defense training. The 75th Ranger Regiment requires the specialized combat emergency skills of a Ranger Medic, a specifically trained 91B Medical Specialist. The Ranger Regiment relies upon its medic's training in trauma and military medicine. The Special Operations Medical Training Battalion graduates all special operations medics, regardless of service branch. The training takes them from military field environments to civilian inner-city hospital trauma centers and prepares them to handle all types of injuries and illnesses— from the common cold to land-mine wounds—and even teaches them to deliver babies. As a member of the 75th Ranger Regiment's fire support team, the Fire Support Specialist (MOS 13F) is specifically knowledgeable of the latest technology and techniques for the employment of fire support assets, and is able to advise Ranger leadership accordingly in both conventional and special operations. Regardless of MOS, those assigned to the 75th Ranger Regiment have opportunities to attend Ranger School, Airborne School, and Pathfinder School. Other advanced military schools specific to their MOS are available, including the Dive Medical Technician Course, Flight Medic Course, Operational and Emergency Skills Course, Special Operations Radio Operator Course, Jumpmaster Course, Battle Staff Course, Technical Escort School, Joint Firepower Control Course, Special Operations Spotter Course, and the Marine Tactical Air Control Party Course.

CHAPTER 4

THE TRAINING CONTINUES

Keeping pressure on the enemy increases the survivability and success rate of the element. When a Ranger makes contact with the enemy listening post and takes out the sentry, the downside is knowing his buddies are nearby and they know the Ranger is approaching. Speed with security and firepower keeps the pressure on.

Ranger Regiment training is chronic and pervasive. It consumes and permeates each individual and the unit on every level. A Ranger knows that in order to embrace wholly the Ranger Creed, professional development is a must. Earning the illustrious Ranger Tab is not the final stop. Individuals expand their skills and knowledge by attending additional schools and training courses. Specific and specialized schools provide greater in-depth training and practical application not provided at the Ranger Battalion or 75th Ranger Regiment level.

One such school called Survival, Evasion, Resistance, Escape (SERE) trains the Rangers to survive off the land if lost or separated from their units. Since Rangers operate behind enemy lines, separation from their units while within enemy territory is possible. SERE School is conducted at the Colonel James N. Rowe Training Facility at Camp MacKall, located near Fort Bragg, North Carolina. The Rangers learned general survival skills to some extent at the Ranger Battalion level, and SERE training provides them with the opportunity to extend and apply survival skills to worldwide

(opposite) The quintessential Ranger is geared up for a mission. His equipment makes him complete. He is equipped with the following: M4A1 rifle with Advanced Combat Optical Gun-sight (ACOG) 4x32 power scope, AN/PEQ-2 infrared target pointer/illuminator/aiming device, M203 grenade launcher, newly designed Modular Integrated Communications Helmet (MICH) headgear, and lightweight internal communications equipment. This Ranger squad leader teaches his men by example and guides them through a blank-fire rehearsal before the live-fire training mission.

Discussing the best way to take an enemy bunker is common practice. Here, Rangers discuss contingency plans in the event that things do not happen according to the plan.

Most Rangers would agree that the accelerated pace and elevated intensity of the training makes time go by quickly in battalion. Few Rangers spend their entire military careers in the Ranger Regiment. Those who are reassigned to another light infantry unit usually have a difficult time adjusting to the slower pace and reduced level of training. Many Rangers spend a portion of their careers as instructors in the Ranger Training Brigade or another specialized school. Still others may apply for another special operations forces assignment.

Colonel "Nick" Rowe, for whom the Colonel James N. Rowe Training Facility is named, survived as a prisoner of war in Vietnam for five years until he escaped from his captors. He was assassinated on April 21, 1989, while serving as a senior advisor for the Joint United States Military Advisory Group to the Philippines. Today he rests at Arlington National Cemetery outside the nation's capitol.

environments. The 19-day school concludes with an evasion exercise in which students experience physical and mental stress that tests their endurance, resolve, and techniques. The self-sufficient and resourceful student is the one most likely to graduate from this course and the one most likely to survive if ever placed in a captive situation.

More specifically, SERE students are taught hand-to-hand combat and tactics to eliminate sentries. Survival tactics include walking at night to conserve fluids, making a solar still to collect water, and leaving visible signals for searchers. The students are taught evasion techniques to avoid possible capture. The school conducts intensive training in support of the Code of Conduct, as upholding the Code of Conduct is paramount as a captured service member. This entails developing mental and emotional strength, both of which are backed by the power of knowledge. Knowing enemy exploitation and political indoctrination tactics provides Rangers with the skills to resist such practices, to circumvent endangering their own

These Rangers have successfully cleared and secured this bunker and now use it as their platform for clearing the following bunker on the operations order. Using an enemy fire position reduces exposure to enemy fire from other enemy positions.

A C-17 aircraft drops Rangers at Fryar Drop Zone at Fort Benning, the place where they originally learned how to jump from an airplane. The Ranger Battalions jump from C-130, C-141, and C-17 aircraft. Airborne insertion occurs from a variety of helicopters.

Rangers from the 3rd Battalion prepare to board a C-141 aircraft for a jump to clear and secure an airfield. Rangers help one another rig equipment and check proper points of performance. Safety is crucial.

(opposite) Daylight jumps are few and far between for Rangers in the regiment. Night provides concealment for air operations, and they help achieve surprise. Concealment helps protect the Airborne Ranger as he drifts to the drop zone.

survival, and to avoid jeopardizing the military's mission. The school also teaches planning and executing escape from captivity. Tactics and techniques taught at SERE school are drawn from the experiences of past prisoners of war, be they escaped, rescued, or released.

The U.S. Army Pathfinder School trains its students in a variety of skills to prepare them for troops arriving via airborne insertion. The school is three weeks long and is held at Fort Benning, Georgia. Over the course of the modern-day U.S. military's history, Pathfinder units and formalized training courses have come and gone. In 1955, the school was reopened under the Airborne–Air Assault branch of the Infantry School to reestablish training operations. Today's Pathfinder School is available to either enlisted applicants or officers who require Pathfinder skills, usually those with an MOS related to infantry, aviation, scouts, or communications. All Pathfinder School students need a valid Pathfinder physical and must be cleared to participate in airborne operations. Pathfinder School candidates must not have any speech impediments, as Pathfinders must verbally communicate vital

Learning the eight survival techniques in SERE school will increase the chances of staying alive and returning to friendly forces. Each student must live by his wits while taking into account his surroundings, physical condition, and available equipment and resources. These eight techniques are easily remembered in this way:

S	Size up the situation
U	Undue haste makes waste
R	Remember where you are
V	Vanquish fear and panic
I	Improvise
V	Value living
A	Act like the natives
L	Learn basic skills

information to the commanders of arriving troops. Unclear communication could compromise the mission.

Today's Pathfinders are trained in airborne, small boat, vehicle, foot, and sometimes free-fall infiltration techniques. Pathfinders may be expected to coordinate aircraft movement, control parachute drops of personnel and equipment, conduct sling-load operations, and provide initial weather information to commanders. Students hone their navigational skills both with and without the use of modern technology. Furthermore, they provide basic air traffic control techniques and navigational assistance to airborne operations. Pathfinder

A mass tactical jump is the beginning of the mission. Those with crew-served weapon systems are the first to exit the aircraft since they are the most effective in fighting the enemy. In the event that the aircraft takes on fire and the "stick" must cease exiting, those with crew-served weapons can hold their own alone.

students establish, mark, and operate helicopter landing and parachute drop zones for the daytime and nighttime. They survey the site and provide security. They learn drop-zone marking techniques to prepare for the arriving airborne troops. The Pathfinder must communicate to the aviator the proper information so the parachutists are released over the drop zone at the appropriate time. Release of the airborne personnel is dependent on wind speed, weather, drop-zone area, and number of personnel and aircraft. Therefore, the Pathfinder student must know how and when to use the computed air-release points

A sniper class is briefed by an instructor prior to a stalking exercise. The students will low-crawl several hundred yards to avoid "compromise" by the Sniper School instructor, who is using an aiming scope. If a student is detected, he must begin again. In some cases, this exercise consumes a great amount of time. Impatience will get a student nowhere. Route reconnaissance plays a vital role in survivability.

U.S. Army Sniper School produces highly lethal sharpshooters. Camouflage techniques are taught, and snipers design their own Ghillie suits to disguise their presence in a specific environment. Ghillie suits were developed by Scottish game wardens during the 19th century to catch poachers.

(CARPs), the ground-marking release system, the Army Aircraft Verbal Initiated Release System, and the PIBALL weather balloon, which measures the mean effective wind. Near the course's end, students participate in a three-day FTX as a member of a Pathfinder Team and in the graded positions of team leader and assistant team leader.

Special Operation Target Interdiction Course (SOTIC) is more commonly referred to as Sniper School. The mission of the U.S. Army SOTIC is to train the volunteers to engage selected point targets with precision rifle fire from long-range and concealed positions. Sniper School attendance is open to more than the Ranger Regiment; however, those designated as snipers within the Ranger Company's rifle squad must be graduates of this school. The school is open to those with an applicable infantry, cavalry scout, or special forces MOS and who are also enlisted in active duty, reserve, or national guard units. Most attendees are from the Ranger Regiment or special forces "Green Beret" units. Commanders must recommend the candidates. A sniper school candidate must have a good performance record without a history of alcohol or drug abuse. He must have passed several stringent psychological evaluations by a qualified examiner. Secret clearance is required. He must be physically fit, as shown by scores of 70 percent or better in each event on the APFT. Corrected vision of 20/20 and normal color vision are requirements. He must be knowledgeable of all infantryman operating procedures, have a GT score of 100, and have been qualified as an "expert" with his rifle within the six months prior to course attendance.

During this six-week course at Fort Bragg, North Carolina, students are taught advanced rifle marksmanship and sniper marksmanship with the M24 Sniper Weapon System, a single-shot, bolt-action rifle with a 7.62-millimeter

> Sniper school students are trained experts in their weapon system and are familiar with various other U.S. and foreign sniper weapon systems. The small class size of less than 25 students and the low instructor-to-student ratio of 1:4 are paramount in precision training. SOTIC graduates are infinitely precise. At a distance of 2,000 meters, snipers can hit the targeted personnel standing immediately beside a noncombatant.

A Sniper School instructor conducts an After Action Review (AAR) with the class, then sets forth a brief time schedule for upcoming events.

The eye of a sniper is one of his most important assets. Snipers work in pairs, with each pair comprised of a spotter and a shooter. The senior ranking or more experienced man is the spotter, and he is the one who identifies targets, assesses wind direction and speed, calculates distance, and records hit information on the target after the shot is taken.

round. This rifle has an estimated maximum effective range of 800 meters (about 875 yards). The M24 rifle, with its sling, daytime optic sight, and a full magazine, weighs just over 14 pounds. The weight of the complete weapon system is approximately 64 pounds. Sniper students learn to integrate available technology by using the rifle with its scope, a spotting scope, binoculars, and night-vision equipment. The students learn to camouflage themselves and their equipment, and master skills like concealed movement, observation techniques, target detection, field craft, and range estimation. These key skill areas, when combined with expert marksmanship, insure maximum engagement of targets.

The most common reason for a missed shot by a sniper is incorrect estimation of the distance to the target. Accurate range-estimation is one of the most important skills a sniper should possess, therefore training in the various range estimation techniques and in the use of laser range-finders is vitally important. These estimation techniques include the map method, 100-meter method, appearance of object method, bracketing method, range card method, and use of the mil relation formula. A sniper must continuously search his engagement area for target indicators. Target indicators include sound, movement, odor, improper camouflage, disturbance of wildlife, or anything else the target does that discloses its position and attracts the sniper's attention.

Instructors conduct exercises in stalking and counter-stalking. During one exercise, they carefully watch with binoculars and range finders for signs that point to the sniper's position. The snipers who can stealthily approach the instructor without being detected pass the exercise. On another exercise, students are airborne inserted and then move over land to approach the instructors for a "shot." They must score a hit on the first attempt to graduate.

Airborne is characteristic of Ranger operations. It is the jumpmaster aboard the aircraft who coordinates and oversees the process of getting Rangers and equipment out the aircraft's door. The mission of the U.S. Army Jumpmaster School is to train personnel in the skills necessary to coordinate and execute a combat-equipped airborne insertion. This entails the proper attaching, jumping, and releasing of combat and individual equipment and personnel. To achieve Jumpmaster status, one must demonstrate a high degree of proficiency in the Jumpmaster Personnel Inspection (JMPI). Students accomplish this by inspecting three rigged jumpers within five minutes and obtaining a minimum score of 70 percent without missing major deficiencies. Jumpmaster students must also successfully complete an actual jump with airborne paratroopers and equipment.

The U.S. Military Free-Fall Parachutists Course is a four-week course at Fort Bragg, North Carolina, designed to teach the appropriate special operations forces personnel, Department of Defense, and foreign personnel the skills for high-altitude airborne operations. More commonly known as HALO School, this course is for those who truly love falling through the skies.

Training begins on the ground. During the first week, the students learn about the MTI-XX parachute, a highly modified, civilian, ram-air chute that can glide at airspeeds of up to 25 miles per hour. For the high-altitude portion of HALO School, student jumpers learn about the oxygen system as well as how to breathe from two compressed oxygen "bailout bottles." The school covers jump commands as well as emergency, rigging, and repack procedures. Practice on the ground always precedes the application of these skills in the air. Each student is strapped into a hanging harness to practice emergency procedures such as malfunctions, cutaways, and entanglements. Training also covers advanced aircraft procedures, including individual exits with and without combat equipment, mass exits, and grouping exercises. Students learn and practice body stabilization in the Vertical Wind Tunnel, which simulates free fall while still utilizing every safety precaution. This apparatus includes an enormous fan blowing at speeds up to 150 miles per hour, creating wind strong enough to lift and support most adults.

The spotter communicates important information to the shooter. Here, the sniper team takes turns marking rounds in preparation for a graded firing that will take place the following day.

For the next three weeks, students spend nearly all their time jumping. On the initial jumps, the parachutist exits at an altitude of 10,000 feet without equipment. The series of jumps concludes with a jump from an altitude of 25,000 feet with full equipment and oxygen. To be safe, the maximum an equipped jumper can weigh when exiting the aircraft is 360 pounds. The student must maintain body stability, deploy his parachute at the designated altitude, and land within 25 meters of the group leader. The school also conducts night-time operations and jumps. The free-fall parachutist student makes at least fourteen jumps, but if the weather is cooperative, more jumps are made, including High Altitude High Opening (HAHO) jumps.

HALO is a means of troop insertion. Its goal is to avoid detection by having men jump from an altitude of up to 25,000

The HALO jumper's ram-air parachute is square in shape, unlike the round canopy parachute used in the Basic Airborne Course, or Jump School. The ram-air chute behaves more like a wing and is more maneuverable in comparison to its rounded counterpart. The ram-air canopy is manually deployed by a rip cord, although all jumpers are equipped with an automatic opening device, which deploys the chute should the jumper become unable to do it himself. Round canopies are extracted by static lines, are less maneuverable, and can support greater weight. Usually, the jumper hits the ground a bit harder with the round canopy.

feet, then free fall to about 200 feet above the ground before opening the canopy. HAHO also dodges detection and keeps the aircraft out of harm's way. The HAHO parachutists pull the ripcord a few seconds after exiting the aircraft, then glide

A sniper's attention to detail results in success. The sniper must be keenly knowledgeable and aware of the environment. All five sensory avenues are on alert to both detect and remain undetected. Some snipers avoid eating certain foods that may emit strong smells later.

Students low-crawl, high-crawl, and observe noise and light discipline. They stealthily approach the instructors. The belly or front side of the Ghillie suit is smooth and absent of pockets so the sniper's clothing will not snag on the ground as he low-crawls. It also allows for a fluid, quiet movement. At the end of a stalking exercise, students are ordered to show themselves.

several miles to the drop zone. Normally, a chest-mounted, magnetic compass guides HAHO jumpers to the drop zone; however, more recently, jumpers have begun to use compact GPS satellite navigation units. In HALO and HAHO jumps, rucksacks are strapped around the jumpers' thighs, where they remain during descent, then are kicked loose when the parachutists are about ten feet from the ground.

For the qualified individual who thrives on the thrill of free-fall, there is Military Free-Fall Jumpmaster training. The free-fall jumpmaster's skills include implementation of altimeters and automatic ripcord-release devices, canopy control, emergency procedures, oxygen procedures, wind drift calculations, and rigging techniques. Responsibilities

include supervising the rigging of individual main parachutes and equipment.

The U.S. Army Combat Diver's School or Combat Diver Qualification Course (CDQC) is best known as Scuba School. This four-week school is one of the tougher schools the army has to offer. Scuba School's objective is to train personnel to be qualified military combat divers. These divers perform water operations that include daytime and nighttime ocean dives, deep dives, and open-circuit swims. Students are evaluated on 1,500- and 3,000-meter navigation dives. To achieve such water operations, the divers must learn diving physics, dive tables, and submarine lock-in/lock-out procedures, and have an understanding of tides

A Ranger sniper team can engage targets from a distance of 1,000 meters with pinpoint and deadly accuracy. The Barrett M82A1 is a semi-automatic, .50-caliber sniper rifle. During the Civil War, Hiram Berdan of the Union forces and Robert E. Lee of the Confederates were the first in history to set up units of designated sharpshooters. The first U.S. Army Sniper School was operated during the Korean War from 1954 to 1955 by the Army Marksmanship Unit (AMU). The current U.S. Army Sniper School was established in 1987.

Snipers from the 1st Ranger Battalion armed with the M24 rifle conduct a reconnaissance mission prior to the Rangers' fast-rope insertion to secure the objective. Snipers are able to identify enemy vehicles, aircraft, and weapon systems, then relay this important information to the commander.

An Airborne Ranger does not want to remember that he forgot how to do something while he is in the air with the land approaching quickly. Sustained Airborne Training is a refresher course held prior to each jump to review the "how-to" and the "what-if" questions. These 3rd Battalion Rangers practice checking the canopy and gaining canopy control.

and currents, potential injuries, and marine hazards. The school also covers first aid and CPR. The school added its Water Infiltration Course (WIC) in more recent years, which consists of Zodiac operations and navigation, numerous surface swims, FTX, Klepper operations, and waterproofing-gear.

Scuba School is open to commissioned officers, warrant officers, or enlisted members of active or reserve duty and to selected Department of Defense personnel assigned to a special operations forces unit. After being screened and recommended by their sending unit's commander, Scuba School candidates arrive for the entrance examination. Requirements for entrance include an APFT minimum of 70 points in each event and an overall score of 210 or above using the APFT's 17- to 21-year-old age group requirements scale. Entrants must swim nonstop on the surface for 500 meters using only the breaststroke or sidestroke and swim 25 meters underwater without breaking the water's surface with any part of the body. They must tread water for two minutes continuously with both hands and ears out of the water. Finally, students must retrieve a 20-pound weight from a depth of 3 meters.

Scuba School divers spend time in the classroom and the pool, but the majority of their time is spent in the crystal clear waters of Key West, Florida. To remain in the course, divers must pass all exercises and navigational dives. The exercise called "Ditching and Donning" takes place in the pool. The divers must swim underwater to the deep end, remove their

face masks, snorkels, and fins, and leave their twin tanks on the pool's floor, placing the weight belts on top of them. Divers then take one breath of compressed air, surface, breathe, and return to the bottom of the pool. They must then put on all of their equipment and begin using the compressed air. Another exercise is the "Harassment Dive." The students swim around the pool's bottom edge and get "harassed" by instructors. Facemasks are pulled, fins are removed, and the divers are basically tormented for up to an hour.

The Ranger's intense training schedule occurs at the battalion, company, platoon, and squad level. The technique of "learning by doing" could better be described as "rehearse, rehearse, rehearse, and rehearse—and execute." Frequent review is provided as a safety measure as well as a way to insure knowledge and understanding.

Sustained airborne training is just one example of ongoing training. This refresher session takes place on the ground and prior to the jump with Airborne Ranger personnel. The jumpmaster or qualified personnel reviews actions in the aircraft, making sure students know everything from what to do in case of a fire to how to deploy the reserve chute both with and without the aircraft's door open. They also review the jump commands as well as the mishaps that could take place in the air—like entanglements, twisted risers, mid-air collisions, or getting caught in a tree.

Rangers conduct airborne jumps as a "refresher" in conjunction with field training and other exercises. While still

on the ground, the initial "manifest call" is made. This serves as a type of roll call and allows the first sergeant to verify how many Rangers will jump out of the plane. The final manifest call double-checks who will be on the plane and usually takes place on the ground as the men are rigging up. Everyone checks identification cards and dog tags. For safety, they also inspect the Kevlar helmets for impact liners and chin-straps. Sometimes, the Rangers rig up for the jump while "in flight," especially if it is a long flight to the drop zone. The jumpmaster conducts his inspection of the airborne personnel, and once he has done this, the parachutist cannot remove any of his rigging without a recheck.

The C-130 and C-141 aircraft are loud. The noise aboard them is deafening, and the movement is jarring. Many Rangers allow the engines' drone to lull them asleep. Others cannot sleep with the engines roaring. All are jolted to attention when the jumpmaster loudly calls the jump commands over the din. Automatically, the Rangers get to their feet and respond.

(above) The green light goes on. A mass tactical jump means many men jump in much equipment. The equipment is compactly packed into their rucksacks. Larger pieces are secured to pallets and air dropped. Weapons are secured to their bodies. They bring everything they will need for the exercise. Any space-saving and weight-reducing measures are taken. Rangers will "strip" their MREs by removing extra cardboard packaging as well as the items they do not eat. When they land, they are ready for anything. These 3rd Battalion Rangers jump from 1,200 feet to land in a sheep field along the German countryside.

On the ramp of a C-130, Rangers from the 75th Ranger Regiment Reconnaissance Detachment (Team 3) conduct HALO operations. They are the eyes and ears of the Ranger Regiment Headquarters element. These highly schooled teams report enemy activity and strength prior to the arrival of the main body of Ranger assault. Each RRD team is assigned to one of the three battalions. Usually the team members have served in that battalion prior to RRD assignment.

Not only are the RRD teams HALO-qualified, but also SCUBA-qualified, and they usually are an E-6 rank or higher. In more recent times, the RRD teams have participated in real-world missions in the Baltic, reporting border violations and collecting activity information for the United Nations.

PT occurs five days a week in Ranger Battalion. If the squad is young, or "cherries," PT may even occur six days a week and on holidays. One 1st Battalion Ranger recalls PT during his early days at battalion. "We were coming in from our pre-dawn run as other guys were dragging in from their late Friday night on the town," he recounted. Rangers as a whole have higher scores on the AFPT than any other unit in the army. This 2nd Battalion Ranger pushes himself to the point of complete muscular fatigue.

The Fast-Rope Infiltration Exfiltration System (FRIES) quickly delivers large numbers of Rangers from rotary-wing aircraft, such as the Blackhawk and Chinook helicopters. Abbreviated by the name "fast-roping," it is much like sliding down a firehouse pole. The difference is that this pole is actually 40, 60, or 80 feet of thick, composite nylon rope. The soldiers' gloved hands must act as the brakes. The "crawl-walk-run" training method starts on the battalion's 50-foot, fixed-platform, fast-rope tower, where all Rangers demonstrate their abilities under increasingly heavy combat loads, both during the day and at night. From there, training moves to the airfield, where the ropes are suspended from different types of helicopters. Rangers demonstrate what they have mastered by fast-roping with equipment from helicopters into water, onto a field, and onto rooftops. Finally, Rangers fast-rope during live-fire training exercises.

Training extends beyond specialized schools. Operations within the urban environment have increasingly become a focus of training. Military experts in urban terrorism and civil disorder forecast that combat in urbanized areas is unavoidable. Therefore, urban areas are the modern-day battlefields.

Urban combat is precise. Rangers train to defeat an enemy that is interspersed with non-combatants while at the same time limiting civilian casualties and collateral damage. Urban environment operations requiring precision include specific raids, small precise strikes, and small-scale personnel seizure as well as recovery operations like hostage rescues. In many instances, a combination of special operations forces, such as members of Delta Force, Navy SEAL teams, and Special Forces A-teams, conducts these operations in a cooperative effort.

Rangers from the 3rd Ranger Battalion battle those from the 1st Battalion in a tug-of-war match—a match of brute strength and indomitable willpower. In this instance, 1st Battalion out-pulled the 3rd Battalion. When the regiment assembles at Fort Benning for a change of command, the Rangers engage in three days of competition between the battalions, called Ranger Rendezvous. Events include boxing, AFPT, soccer, and football. The event is capped off by a barbecue of mammoth proportions for the entire regiment as well as families and friends.

At Hunter Army Airfield, 1st Battalion Rangers pulling HMMWVs are not an uncommon sight. To maintain interest, squad leaders keep physical training fresh and creative. Such an activity is an actual part of squad competitions between the companies.

The lessons learned from combat demonstrate that although urban operations generally have a slower pace and tempo, they can rapidly deteriorate with little or no forewarning. It is quite possible for a force involved in a support role to suddenly find itself in a highly intense combat situation. Rangers train to expect the unexpected, and the unexpected is highly likely in an urban environment. Military able to understand and follow all directed commands and must not be allowed the means to resist. This poses a challenge as civilians may not speak English, may be hiding, or may be dazed from an explosive device known as a breach, or "flash/bang." Without ever compromising the safety of fellow students, Rangers practice how clearing and search teams will react to these variables.

In squad competitions, members of the 1st Ranger Battalion lug a fully saturated poncho raft out of the water. Activities and competitions foster unity and teamwork within the squad. Securing a poncho around rucksacks creates this raft. It remains afloat as the squad swims and tows it across 175 yards of pond water at Hunter Army Airfield, Georgia.

maps may not provide enough detail for urban terrain analysis, nor may they reflect the underground sewer systems, subways, water systems, or mass transit routes. To complicate things further, reconnaissance is more difficult in this environment.

Strict rules of engagement are established prior to an urban operation and are reviewed frequently. Rangers must have the discipline to distinguish enemies from non-combatants. This is especially difficult to do when enemies and civilians look alike and dress similarly. Civilians must be

Rangers, with their combat experience and the knowledge they acquired in the training environment, often participate in Military Operations on Urbanized Terrain (MOUT). Many of the key MOUT principles mirror the Ranger principles of operation, making Ranger units ideal for urban operations and missions. The element of surprise is the first MOUT principle, as the force strives to strike the enemy at a time and place and in a manner the enemy could not anticipate. Second, units maintain security during all phases of the operation, in all directions, and for the force's (pages 142-143) A Ranger squad from 3rd Ranger Battalion runs toward the sunrise during early morning PT. During daylight-saving time, Rangers see the sunrise more than the sunset. Before commencing this run, the squad leader states the task, condition, and standard the squad must achieve. The distance will be roughly 10 miles set at the leader's pace.

(right) Physical conditioning takes place in times of peace to prepare for combat operations in the future. Many Rangers implement a personal physical training regime in addition to the squad's PT.

Everywhere a Ranger turns, he encounters another training exercise. The 1st Battalion Rangers raid an objective with the support of the M240G machine guns, Carl Gustav, and .50-caliber machine guns, which are off-loaded from an MH-47 Chinook. In an actual combat situation, the AC-130 Spectre gunship would answer the call for fire and hit the objective as the Rangers withdraw from the area.

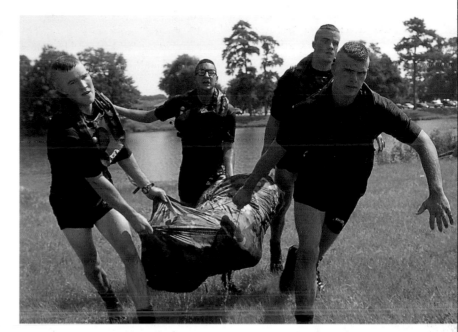

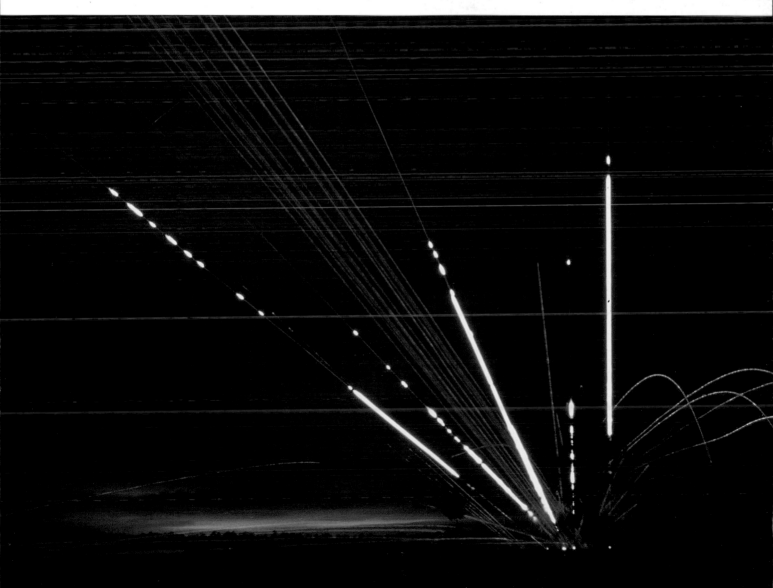

duration in the urban environment. The Rangers work to never permit the enemy to acquire an unexpected advantage or employ its own element of surprise. Third, the MOUT force plans and prepares for the worst, and rehearses everything. It develops clear, concise, uncomplicated plans to ensure everyone's understanding. Next, the rate of military action is paramount. The force moves in a "careful hurry" and never moves faster than it can accurately engage targets. Strong force combined with high speed yields surprise and greatly reduces the opportunity for physical and mental enemy reaction.

For the Ranger, close-quarters combat (CQC) begins with psychological preparation. A Ranger's reaction evolves to the level of instinctual action. In order to survive a close-quarters engagement, Rangers must make quick, accurate rifle shots by mere reflex and continue firing until the enemy target is neutralized. Success and survival in a CQC situation depend primarily on who hits first and puts the other individual down. The Ranger must be proficient in basic rifle marksmanship, for it is this proficiency, not a mastery of

A forward observer (FO) checks the targets, as the live-fire exercise for the mortars section is about to begin. The FO uses Steiner binoculars to watch the action. The mortars section is placed about 400 yards away and cannot see its intended targets.

(above) A raid's power is initiated by the most casualty-producing weapon systems. In this case, the 84-millimeter Carl Gustav fires a HEAT (High Explosive Anti-Tank) round at bunkers on the objective. The Carl Gustav replaces the once popular 90-millimeter recoilless rifle.

As part of a training exercise, 2nd Battalion Rangers from Fort Lewis, Washington, fast-rope from an UH-60 DAP- version Blackhawk helicopter onto the rooftop to secure the building. While the Rangers fast-rope down the cable, the door gunners fire at enemy locations with 7.62-millimeter mini-guns. Bullet shells spill from the helicopter and to the ground below.

advanced skills or higher technology, that results in survival in the urban environment.

Room-clearing procedures are not set in stone. Rangers establish techniques and standard operating procedures within their units. They may need to modify standard operating procedures depending on the urban environment and the given rules of engagement. For instance, to address the possibility of non-combatants in the room, Rangers may use a flash/bang inside a fragmentation grenade. Additionally, the urban environment, by its very nature, presents numerous variables that may or may not fluctuate at any given moment. Rangers rehearse how to negotiate and clear the urban environment's physical structures, which include entryways and their rooms, adjoining rooms, open and closed stairways, hallways, and hallway intersections. In every given room, each Ranger is assigned a specific sector. If a man goes down or his weapon malfunctions, another Ranger takes over his sector of fire.

Although there are a few options once the men are inside the room, there is one technique that is the safest and most recommended for the Ranger unit's clearing team. The Ranger holds the weapon with the butt stock in the pocket of the shoulder and the firing-side elbow tucked in against the body. The weapon's barrel is pointed down so the front sight post and day optic are barely out of the Ranger's field of vision. The Ranger maintains a comfortable boxer stance

with his head up so he can identify targets. Weapon malfunctions do occur, and Rangers must be prepared with well-rehearsed procedures to quickly address such occurrences during CQC. During any CQC training, Rangers practice weapon-malfunction drills within the CQC encounter until procedures are second nature. They do the same with room-clearing drills.

The Joint Readiness Training Center (JRTC) at Fort Polk, Louisiana, houses the MOUT complex, which boasts a one-of-a-kind, state-of-the-art training center. Consisting of three facilities, a mock city, an airfield facility, and a military compound, the MOUT complex trains soldiers to conduct urban environment missions while minimizing or eliminating civilian casualties and collateral damage. The purpose of the complex is to provide realistic training in third-world and urban warfare scenarios and to expand the training foundation for light-infantry and special operations forces. Each Ranger Battalion attends at least one JRTC rotation annually.

In a combat situation, special operations forces such as Rangers depend on the U.S. Air Force for airlift, close air support (CAS), and resupply. Rangers can expect to operate with heavy armor units equipped with tanks and armored personnel carriers. JRTC exercises integrate the special operations forces with air force, other military units, and civilian personnel to replicate nearly realistic scenarios. To intensify the real-world

MH-6 Little Birds from Task Force 160 support Ranger missions with transportation and support fire. The MH-6 drops off Rangers in a tight space with speed and accuracy. Unlike its sister bird, the AH-6, armaments are minimal. The Rangers provide security with their individual weapons as they approach the objective.

(above) After the MH-6 drops off the 2nd Battalion Rangers, it leaves the area until extraction is needed. Rangers run to their assigned buildings and practice clearing them.

(opposite) At Fort Benning, 3rd Battalion Rangers fast-rope into a clearing on a field. Fast-roping is an expedient method of placing numerous Rangers onto a small objective.

The MOUT complex is set up to resemble an actual battlefield, complete with realistic furniture in buildings, props, and civilians. The villagers perform routine civilian activities with vehicles, animals, and private property. Some pose as media. They wear civilian clothes with a MILES harness, but little indicates whether the villager is a combatant or noncombatant. These civilians are integrated into the scenario just as the Rangers may encounter them in an actual urban combat environment, meaning they serve as either shields for sensitive areas or as "targeting" dilemmas. This allows Rangers to apply the Rules of Engagement.

Urban warfare is more likely now than in any other time in our history. Rangers from 3rd Battalion use simunitions to better approximate real-world training. The simunition is a 9-millimeter paint bullet that comes in various colors—red, yellow, blue, neon green. It is available in other calibers as well. Its plastic casing compresses upon impact to cushion the force upon contact. MILES equipment emits a laser beam to a receiver that triggers a noise so you know you have been hit. You know that you have been hit by simunition by the sound of your own yell. For instructional purposes, industries have combined MILES equipment with simunitions.

training experience, the 1st Battalion (Airborne), 509th Infantry, serves as the opposing force for the light-infantry and special operations forces. This force-on-force training, with implementation of the Multiple Integrated Laser Engagement System (MILES), can be conducted throughout the MOUT complex. Continually, the U.S. Military improves its MOUT training facility to enhance the realism. The MOUT training exercises not only enhance the technical and tactical proficiencies of individual soldiers, teams, and units, but also improve the armed services as a whole.

Shughart-Gordon site is a mock city housing 29 buildings in covering a 4.3-square mile (7-square kilometer) area. It was named after two Delta Force operators and

Medal of Honor recipients who died during Operation Restore Hope in Somalia while defending an MH-60 Blackhawk crash site. This mock city includes a church, hospital, several multistory buildings, and an underground tunnel or sewer system. The military can conduct air assault and fast-rope operations within this site. Four live-fire buildings permit platoon-size, live-fire training with Short Range Training Ammunition (SRTA), simunitions (simulated ammunition rounds), or plastic paint bullets. The city's water tower acts as a command and control facility and observation platform.

The second site is Self Airfield, a seven-building airfield facility with a warehouse, air traffic control tower, flight

Close-quarters combat (CQC) training is conducted in the Shoot House, a cinderblock building with sandbagged walls to keep bullets and fragments from penetrating the walls. When the Ranger enters a room, he has less than two seconds to assess the threat level and determine if the people present are noncombatants or combatants.

A class on different breaching techniques is now in session. The "newbees" experience the practical application immediately after instruction. This class concentrates on cutting through a chain-linked fence on the perimeter of an enemy compound. The cutting saw is similar to a regular chainsaw, with a blade for cutting metal. While away from the fence and in the prone position, the Ranger starts up the saw, runs to the fence, then quickly cuts through the chain-link in one downward, sweeping motion. The fence is breached.

landing strip, and additional buildings. The military conducts airborne and air assault operations here. The flight landing strip is a 4,300-foot active runway that can accommodate large aircraft. This airfield is located about 1.9 miles (about 3 kilometers) northwest of the city complex.

Word Military Compound is a five-building site that includes a drill field, barracks, stockade, and guard towers. This compound is about .6 miles (1 kilometer) south of the city site.

The JRTC personnel tailor each exercise to the training goals established by the commander of each unit attending JRTC training. A particular exercise or rotation lasts for approximately two weeks and simulates a U.S. task force helping a small, mythical island nation face an invading military force. Extensive planning and preparation precede the rotation's initial phase. During the first phase and several days prior to the arrival of heavy armored forces, the Rangers arrive by air to conduct operations against the opposing force in a simulated combat setting.

The Observer/Controller (O/C) personnel from the JRTC staff conduct a periodical AAR throughout JRTC training. The O/C personnel control computerized targets, and audiovisual systems are controlled from an administrative facility that includes an AAR theater. The AAR provides the unit with feedback in four important areas. First, the

AAR establishes the key facts of what happened in a combat engagement, why it occurred, and how to fix the problems. Next, soldiers are given the opportunity to recall how the situation developed and discuss the possible alternatives. Third, the AAR format encourages growth and promotes both individual and collective learning. The interactive process of the AAR fosters individual responsibility for actions and professional development, as the unit is depending on each individual. Finally, the AAR paves an avenue for O/Cs to provide guidance and to teach the best doctrinal methods for combat urban environments. Each unit takes the AAR information back to its parent unit to continue the training process.

MILES is a one of many laser-based devices the JRTC uses to promote realistic force-on-force training. It simulates the combative result of several direct-fire weapons by producing "casualties." Each soldier is equipped with a MILES transmitter on his weapon and a MILES receiver. The transmitter emits a laser beam each time a blank round is fired from the attached weapon. Laser transmitters are programmed for each specific weapon system to replicate actual ranges and lethality of that weapon accurately. Information contained in the laser beam includes the soldier's identification and the weapon system used. The soldiers' receivers read the laser beam "bullets." All hits and near misses are indicated by a distinctive audio tone that can only be silenced by a controller's special key. MILES receivers are also placed on all equipment and vehicles within the battlefield arena. All activity is recorded during an exercise, resulting in valuable information for the AAR. MILES training has been proven to dramatically increase the combat readiness and effectiveness of military forces.

RANGERS LEAD THE WAY!

(above) Special Operations Air Force MH-53J Pave Low helicopter arrives with the support element of 1st Battalion's raid. The Pave Low approaches the objective as the mini-guns' door gunners and .50-caliber tail gunner provides cover. In the background, the AH-6J helicopters support the mission.

(right) Ready to go, a 1st Battalion medic prepares to move his injured comrade. Although every safety precaution is taken, injuries occur. For the medic, the training cannot get any more real than this.

(following page) Cathedral of Saint John the Baptist in Savannah, Georgia, is home of the 1st Ranger Battalion. The battalion respectfully lowers its head to honor the memory of three fallen comrades lost in Afghanistan.

Appendix A

Past to Present Commanders and Command Sergeant Majors of the 75th Ranger Regiment

75th Ranger Regiment Commanders

Colonel Wayne A. Downing
Colonel Joseph S. Stringham
Colonel Wesley B. Taylor, Jr.
Colonel William F. Kernan
Colonel David L. Grange
Colonel James T. Jackson
Colonel William F. Leszczynski
Colonel Stanley A. McChrystal
Colonel P. Kenneth Keen
Colonel Joseph L. Votel

75th Ranger Regiment Command Sergeant Majors

Command Sergeant Major Gary Carpenter
Command Sergeant Major Autrail Cobb
Command Sergeant Major George Mock
Command Sergeant Major Mariano Leon-Guerrero
Command Sergeant Major Jesse Laye
Command Sergeant Major George Ponder
Command Sergeant Major Michael Hall
Command Sergeant Major Walter Rakow

Appendix B

75th Ranger Regiment and Battalion Chain of Command

75th Ranger Regiment, Fort Benning, GA

Colonel Joseph L. Votel
Command Sergeant Major Walter E. Rakow

1st Ranger Battalion, 75th Ranger Regiment
Hunter Army Airfield, GA
Lieutenant Colonel Raymond A. Thomas, III
Command Sergeant Major Douglas M. Greenway

2nd Ranger Battalion, 75th Ranger Regiment
Fort Lewis, WA
Lieutenant Colonel Kevin C. Owens
Command Sergeant Major Hugh A. Roberts

3rd Ranger Battalion, 75th Ranger Regiment
Fort Benning, GA
Lieutenant Colonel Stefan J. Banach
Command Sergeant Major Jay A. Brimstin

Appendix C

Ranger School Awards

As delineated in the U.S. Army's Ranger School Course description, the Ranger School awards are as follows:

William O. Darby Award

The Darby Award winner is the top Distinguished Honor Graduate. The recipient has the highest peers, most positive spot reports, and the best performance in both tactical and administrative leadership positions. He must have clearly demonstrated himself as being a cut above all other Rangers. He is recommended by the battalion commanders and Brigade S3 after review of all academic records. Final approval authority is the brigade commander. A Ranger class is not required to have a William O. Darby Award recipient. There is only one William O. Darby Award recipient per class.

Distinguished Honor Graduate

There is one Distinguished Honor Graduate per class. This award goes to the officer or enlisted Honor Graduate with the best overall performance. The recipient is recommended by the battalion commanders and Brigade S3. The brigade commander is the final approving authority for Distinguished Honor Graduate. If none of the students in a category, officer or enlisted, meet the Honor Graduate criteria, the one student in that category with the best overall performance record is designated the Honor Graduate for that category. In this case, there is no Distinguished Honor Graduate.

Ralph Puckett Award

Criteria used to select the Ralph Puckett Awardee (Officer) of the Ranger Course include: Meet the course graduation criteria; pass all graded leadership positions; pass all peer reports; lose no major items of equipment due to negligence (as evidenced by spot reports); have all unsatisfactory spot reports canceled; receive no recycles, other than for compassionate or medical reasons; and require no re-tests on any critical tasks.

Glenn M. Hall Award

Criteria used to select the Glenn M. Hall Awardee (Enlisted) of the Ranger Course include: Meet the course graduation criteria; pass all graded leadership positions; pass all peer reports; lose no major items of equipment due to negligence (as evidenced by spot reports); have all unsatisfactory spot reports canceled; receive no recycles, other than for compassionate or medical reasons; and require no re-tests on any critical tasks.

Merrill's Marauder Award

Criteria used in selecting one officer and one enlisted man for the Merrill's Marauder Award include: must have passed the land navigation course (no re-tests); must have passed all peer evaluations and have the highest cumulative score. The student who received the highest score in land navigation is selected.

Benjamin Church Leadership Award

Criteria used in selecting one officer and one enlisted man who have demonstrated outstanding leadership through out the entire course include: recommended by all battalion commanders, battalion TACs, and Brigade S3; not have been a recycle for any academic reason, i.e. peers, spots, or patrols; have a positive spot record; and have not been a SOR case at anytime in the course.

Noncommissioned Officer Association Award

Given to the top enlisted graduate of each class regardless of other awards received and is sponsored by the NCOA of Columbus, Georgia.

Van Houten Sub-Chapter Chattahoochee Valley Chapter, Ausa Leadership Award

Given to the best informal leader of each class regardless of other awards.

Appendix D
Honoring Fallen Comrades

This book is to honor the memory of the Rangers from the 1st Ranger Battalion who paid the ultimate sacrifice for their country on March 3, 2002, during Operation Anaconda, Afghanistan.

Recognizing that I volunteered as a Ranger, fully knowing the hazards of my chosen profession, I will always endeavor to uphold the prestige, honor, and high esprit de corps of my Ranger Regiment.

Sergeant Bradley S. Crose

Bradley S. Crose, 22, was from Orange Park, Florida, and volunteered for military service with the U.S. Army on June 6, 1998. On November 20, 1998, he was assigned to the 1st Ranger Battalion, 75th Ranger Regiment, at Hunter Army Airfield, Georgia. He earned his Ranger Tab from Fort Benning, Georgia, and was also a graduate of the Primary Leadership Development Course.

Crose held many positions while assigned to the 1st Ranger Battalion. He was killed while fighting the Taliban and Al-Qaeda during Operation Anaconda, the most intense fighting to date in Operation Enduring Freedom in Afghanistan. He died in combat after enemy gunfire forced down an MH-47 Chinook helicopter in which he and his fellow Rangers were aboard.

Specialist Marc A. Anderson

Marc A. Anderson, 30, was from Brandon, Florida, and vol-unteered for military service with the U.S. Army on July 15, 1998. On March 18, 1999, he was assigned to the 1st Ranger Battalion, 75th Ranger Regiment, at Hunter Army Airfield, Georgia. He earned his Ranger Tab from Fort Benning, Georgia.

Anderson was a machine gunner while assigned to the 1st Ranger Battalion. He was killed while fighting the Taliban and Al-Qaeda during Operation Anaconda, the most intense fighting to date in Operation Enduring Freedom in Afghanistan. He died in combat after enemy gunfire forced down an MH-47 Chinook helicopter in which he and his fellow Rangers were aboard.

Corporal Matthew A. Commons

Matthew A. Commons, 21, was born in Boulder City, Nevada. He volunteered for military service with the U.S. Army on July 7, 2000. On April 4, 2001, he was assigned to the 1st Ranger Battalion, 75th Ranger Regiment, at Hunter Army Airfield, Georgia.

Commons was an M203 grenade launcher gunner while assigned to the 1st Ranger Battalion. He was killed while fighting the Taliban and Al-Qaeda during Operation Anaconda, the most intense fighting to date in Operation Enduring Freedom in Afghanistan. He died in combat after enemy gunfire forced down an MH-47 Chinook helicopter in which he and his fellow Rangers were aboard.

Index

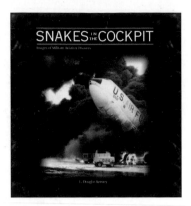

Snakes in the Cockpit: Images
of Military Aviation Disasters
ISBN: 0-7603-1250-8

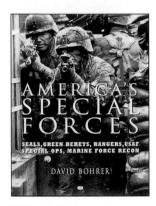

America's Special Forces
ISBN: 0-7603-1348-2

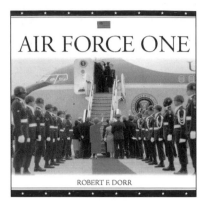

Air Force One
ISBN: 0-7603-1055-6

I Was With Patton
ISBN: 0-7603-1071-8

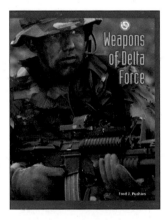

Weapons of Delta Force
ISBN: 0-7603-1139-0

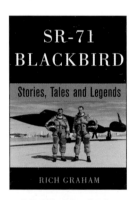

SR-71 Blackbird
Stories, Tales, and Legends
ISBN: 0-7603-1142-0

U.S. Navy SEALs
ISBN: 0-87938-781-5

U.S. Army Special Forces
ISBN: 0-7603-0862-4

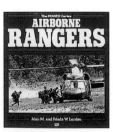

Airborne Rangers
ISBN: 0-87938-606-1